The Enterprising Musician's Guide to Performer Contracts

The Enterprising Musician's Guide to Performer Contracts

DAVID R. WILLIAMS

ROWMAN & LITTLEFIELD
Lanham • Boulder • New York • London

Published by Rowman & Littlefield
A wholly owned subsidiary of The Rowman & Littlefield Publishing Group, Inc.
4501 Forbes Boulevard, Suite 200, Lanham, Maryland 20706
www.rowman.com

Unit A, Whitacre Mews, 26-34 Stannary Street, London SE11 4AB

British Library Cataloguing in Publication Information Available

Library of Congress Cataloging-in-Publication Data
Names: Williams, David R., 1964– author.
Title: The enterprising musician's guide to performer contracts / David R. Williams.
Description: Lanham : Rowman & Littlefield, [2017] | Includes bibliographical
  references and index.
Identifiers: LCCN 2017029338 (print) | LCCN 2017031364 (ebook) |
  ISBN 9781538106778 (electronic) | ISBN 9781538106754 (hardcover : alk. paper) |
  ISBN 9781538106761 (pbk. : alk. paper)
Subjects: LCSH: Musicians' contracts—United States.
Classification: LCC ML3795 (ebook) | LCC ML3795 .W4936 2017 (print) |
  DDC 780.23—dc23
LC record available at https://lccn.loc.gov/2017029338

♾™ The paper used in this publication meets the minimum requirements of American
National Standard for Information Sciences—Permanence of Paper for Printed Library
Materials, ANSI/NISO Z39.48-1992.

Printed in the United States of America

This book is dedicated to creative people everywhere.
It is my hope that the information shared within these pages
will encourage you to embrace the business aspects of your craft
so that the world will continue to benefit from the energy,
passion, and joy that is your gift to the rest of us.

Table of Contents

PART IV: RESOURCES

Foreword

There are many steps on the road to a professional career as a working musician. As students, our paths are specifically laid out before us—prescribed, class by class, as we build up our artistic skill sets. We have guides that lead us through each level: teachers who help us to construct and hone our techniques; teachers for history and theory who provide us context and a framework upon which to hang our individual arts; and conductors, directors, and coaches who supply us with the experiences necessary to make us more autonomous performers, able to look on our music with a discerning eye that enables us to apply the right styles, the correct diction, and an informed interpretation. We learn how to present ourselves, how to audition, and what kind of pieces will serve us best during those auditions. We follow up our university study with summer festivals and apprenticeship programs, building up a curriculum vitae that boasts a level of progress that makes us as attractive a prospect as possible.

As young artists turn into emerging artists, a major shift occurs and the skill set we need broadens considerably. The professional world looms large, and now it is not enough that we know how and what we want to play and with whom. We need to know how to make a living doing it, and how to find the right people to help us on that part of the journey. Taking it to the next level isn't easy—there are so many paths to take, and no one path is the right one for everyone. What it means to be a working musician has changed enormously in the last twenty years, and today, artists need to be more responsible than ever for the trajectory of their own careers. That means understanding their relationship to those that represent them, and their relationship to the companies that hire them. For some artists, it is about knowing how to successfully represent themselves. It means understanding contracts.

I met author David Williams during the summer of 1994, at the Tangle-wood Music Center. David was visiting some mutual friends, and we hit it off immediately. Little did I know that five years later, we would be sharing an apartment on the Upper West Side. I was steadily working at the Metropolitan Opera, making trips to Paris and London and holding my own in a career that was going at a very good pace. David was working in downtown Manhattan (he gives a great account of this part of his life in the preface) and was hard at work on his law degree. What I appreciated about David was the great balance he had in his life with music and with business. No matter what he has been working on, he has always found a way to use his formidable talent and education to enlighten and enhance whatever is before him. Music and his respect and love for those that make it create a lens through which he sees possibilities and answers. It is a balance of head and heart. That is what makes this book so important—he gives artists a different and very important way to look at their work. It provides answers to some very pertinent questions, and as a masterclass teacher and colleague, I have heard these questions over and over. What does it mean to have an agent, a manager? What is the differ-ence between union and non-union contracts? What should I be looking for in a contract with a manager, in a contract with a house? What do I do when something goes awry? What do I do . . . ?

An enterprising artist is someone who wants to get in front of those ques-tions. Every career comes up against obstacles—at every stage of the career. It's just like having a voice. Sometimes things sail along as if nothing could stop you, and then one morning you wake up and you can barely speak. How we handle those issues can make or break us. David Williams wants to be a part of what makes your artistic life easier and forward thinking. As someone who has had the good fortune to get advice from him over the years on an array of subjects, one of the things that draws me to David is the knowledge that he is only interested in being a facilitator—that is his art. He wants to empower musicians by teaching them how to do this work for themselves rather than paying him or someone else to do it for them. This book will serve as a transla-tor, a guide, a template for how you communicate on the business side of your business. It's time.

Glean everything you can from this wonderful information. The book is incredibly user friendly, and takes the time to point out specific areas of caution and presents terrific hints along the way as well. David presents complicated data in a way that is easy for any layperson to understand—step by step, starting with the fundamentals. Don't skip the theory, my friends. It is exactly like studying your instrument: foundation first!

When I spoke with him about this book, I asked David why this was so important to him. His answer: because it is important to know how to be entrepreneurs for music, and to do that, we must be entrepreneurs for ourselves. Once we understand those skills, we need to pass them on to our present and future colleagues. As teachers, we need to "further the dialogue about the imperative for university programs to expand their curricula to include critical, relevant entrepreneurship skills for performance majors because talent alone cannot serve as a basis for a sustainable career." Those are his words, not mine. I wish I had written them because they are spot-on.

Making music is an honor, a joy, a privilege. But we all know that the business of making music can be a mystery that makes the dream a nightmare. There are stumbling blocks, but believe me, books like this one are there to lift the veil. A successful musical life is based on practice, knowledge, imagination, forethought, and action. What are we all taught from the moment we start studying in earnest? Be aware, listen, and be ready for your moment. You never know when the turning point will come for you. Guide yourself with knowledge—it isn't about us versus them, it is about understanding how all the pieces of this crazy puzzle fit together. This book will be invaluable to you in that journey, and if you need any more help, you can always check out David's website: www.EnterprisingArtistConsulting.com.

At the risk of sounding too sentimental—well, it's no risk, really, and I can't help myself—I am so proud of David for making his dream a reality through this wonderful book. He has always been and continues to be a cheerleader and sustaining force in my life as a friend and as a musician, and it thrills me to no end that so many others will benefit from the immense knowledge that he has spent so much time and energy accumulating. It is one thing to understand where there is a need. It is quite another to be the person who fills it by providing answers.

With gratitude,
Stephanie Blythe
Opera singer, recitalist, cabaret performer, teacher

Acknowledgments

I am grateful to all the folks at Rowman & Littlefield for their support for this project, including Katie O'Brien, who prepared the manuscript. Acquisitions editor Natalie Mandziuk immediately understood how important it is for all creative people, not only musicians, to have access to this critical information. I'm thankful to be in such good hands.

I am also indebted to several others who helped bring this book to life, but perhaps to no one more that Stephanie Blythe. Stephanie has been a longtime champion of me, my work, and the ideas contained in this book. I am deeply grateful for her many years of friendship and support and only hope that I haven't inadvertently beguiled her into writing the flattering things she so eloquently presents in her foreword.

Lisa Napoletano's contribution cannot be understated. As with everything she trains her eyes and hands upon, she fully committed herself to the enterprise of editing two manuscript revisions, offering many pages of commentary on my ideas and how I communicate them here.

The following people made direct and valuable contributions, resulting in a book that is easier to use and understand: Michele Bautier, Maureen Coleman, Thomas Cooley, Kirk D. Gardner, Susan Craft Larson, Susan Nackley Mojave, John O'Brien, Kathleen Otterson, Melody Blythe Parker, Debra Patchell, Brian Patterson, Mary C. Peck, Jamie Schmidt, Diane Rae Schoff, and Esther Scott.

Finally, my Music Law students at the Crane Institute for Music Business, through their honest questions about the material and its presentation, provided me with immediate and invaluable feedback.

To each of you, a heartfelt thank you.

Table of Examples

(*by Chapter*)

Chapter Four—Interpreting Contract Language:
Eight Tips for Getting Started

Chapter Five—Clauses Commonly Found in Musicians' Contracts

Chapter Nine—Self-Help

Preface

Congratulations! Holding this book in your hands means that you have taken the first step toward managing your professional future.

After several years as a professional musician and studio voice teacher in the Midwest, I decided to take a big personal and professional risk: I closed my voice studio, leaving behind the professional network that took me years to build, and moved to New York City. I wasn't running from anything specific, but I also wasn't going to anything specific. After earning three degrees in music (including a DMA) before I turned thirty, I needed a break. I needed to try something different, but what?

Like most people who relocate to a major city with little money, I desperately needed to find work and soon had several part-time jobs. I worked as a file clerk temp for an insurance company in the financial district; was a maître d' at a rotating restaurant in Times Square (where I was constantly disoriented); accompanied voice classes at the famed Actors Studio; and worked for an artist manager whose roster included prominent opera singers, pianists, and conductors.

As I had several exceptionally talented friends who were embedded in the city's most prestigious music organizations and performing at its most celebrated venues, I was frequently invited to be a guest at their performances and was meeting world-class musicians. And working for the artist manager gave me access to the behind-the-scenes workings of Manhattan's classical music and musical theater scene. It was thrilling, and I started to see a future for myself in this world—working as either an artist manager or as an arts administrator for one of the larger performing arts organizations.

No matter how it evolved, I knew it would take time. I was enjoying my new (exhausting) life, but a full-time position eluded me despite my networking and interviewing. I continually heard the same thing: "We're not sure you're going to stick around." They thought I was biding my time before returning to academia to be a university voice teacher—an option that no longer interested me.

Soon I was faced with a decision: the insurance company offered me a full-time position with a salary that, at that time, seemed shockingly generous. Accepting the position meant giving up my other jobs—including the ones I enjoyed and hoped would lead me to where I wanted to be. So, after two years of interviewing, constant rejections, no true mentor, and a dwindling number of leads, I accepted the insurance company's offer. It was a hard choice: the money, benefits, and hours were great, but had I made a Faustian bargain?

Within a year, having worked my way up to being an underwriter, I decided to take advantage of my company's tuition reimbursement program. Because everything business-related was still new to me, I started taking short self-study courses to expand my knowledge of finance, insurance, and business law. My interest in law soon eclipsed my interest in the other areas, and I started thinking of law school.

A year later I was an evening division student at New York Law School. In addition to fully supporting my choice to get a law degree, my company also helped pay for it while I worked there! After completing the required portion of my law school coursework, I focused on my personal interests: entertainment law; upper-level contract drafting; intellectual property law, including trademark, service mark, copyright, and patents; media law; and Internet law, which, at that time, was just being settled.

Life was difficult during those years, but I honestly loved it and was fully engaged in what I was doing. I decided I wanted to use this new legal training and my background in music to help musicians and other creative people in some way, but I didn't want to work at a law firm. Graduating at thirty-seven years old, I didn't want the hours, the stress, or to have to start my career over again from the bottom at a law firm. Besides, to my surprise, my insurance career continued to advance while I was in law school.

By graduation I combined my law degree with my experience as an Internet liability underwriter and was hired to work in the insurance practice of a data and analytics company to author an e-commerce insurance policy. I didn't know it at the time, but I was developing a specialty in the drafting and interpretation of complex professional liability contracts, which require knowledge of many of the basic principles of entertainment law.

While I enjoyed the challenges of my work, I wondered if I would ever get back to music or find a way to combine it with business and law. Then, one casual after-dinner conversation with a friend changed everything.

My friend, a stage director, told me that his plans to purchase an engagement ring for his fiancée would be delayed because one of his upcoming jobs was canceled and he had been depending on that income to buy the ring. Here's the gist of our conversation:

Me: Why was the opera production canceled?

He: Budget problems.

Me: Do you have a contract?

He: Yes.

Me: They still have to pay you.

He: But I won't actually be working there, because they shortened the season and canceled my show.

Me: Yes, but they still have to pay you. That's why you have a contract: each party promises something to the other and each has to keep his promise. You promised to reserve time in your schedule for them, which stopped you from accepting work anywhere else during that period. In exchange, they promised to pay you for your time.

He: Well, I did call them and ask what they could do for me, and they said "nothing" because they said the contract has a Force Majeure Clause in it.

Me: Hmm . . . fax the contract to me on Monday and let me look at it.

You'll read about *force majeure* in Chapter 5, but essentially it means an Act of God, such as a hurricane or blizzard, where the non-performance of one or more parties to a contract is excused due to the impossibility of materially complying with the contract's terms. "Budget problems," while very real for non-profits, are *not* Acts of God.

Since his phone call didn't produce results, we decided to write a polite but firm letter asking for his fee. The letter, sent by registered mail, made it clear that he knew his rights, was serious about exercising them, and was keeping good records of his efforts.

After a few weeks he received the money that was due him and he bought the engagement ring.

I felt invincible! This was why I went to law school in the first place—to empower musicians and other creative people to understand their rights and to help them exercise those rights in a businesslike manner.

Soon, I was asked for guidance with several other contract-related issues, including a dispute between the chorus of an award-winning Broadway show and its producers and a breach of contract lawsuit brought against a singer by her manager. And I met several creative people with similar problems as part of my volunteer work at two legal clinics in Manhattan.

It became clear that these creative folks needed some help. After years of collecting contract samples and working in support of artists' rights, I was invited to speak at the New England Conservatory of Music, where I earned my master's degree, on performers' contracts—both presenter's engagement contracts and artist-management contracts. For over a decade now I have been engaged as a guest lecturer on these and related topics at conservatories and professional training programs across the country.

This book is an expanded version of those lectures and what I've learned along the way. It is my sincere hope that you find it useful and user-friendly.

Introduction

All creative people, not just musicians, need to understand the contracts they sign and the binding professional relationships they enter (even if they never sign an actual contract).

Though I wrote this book with musicians in mind, in truth it is relevant to any creative person who provides a service for a fee: musicians, actors, choreographers, directors, writers, performance artists, etc. It will empower you by teaching you a threefold set of skills: (1) how to understand the basics of binding obligations in a contractual relationship (written or otherwise), (2) how to write an effective business letter, and (3) how to know when it's time to seek legal help.

After reading this book you should:

- know what constitutes a valid contract
- understand your rights
- be able to appropriately exercise your rights while preserving the business relationship when a dispute arises

WHY THIS BOOK CANNOT PROVIDE LEGAL ADVICE

This book cannot and does not provide you with legal advice. Legal advice is something very specific. It means that a lawyer has considered the facts relevant to parties in a dispute or other situation, determined which laws apply, and then predicted how a court of law is likely to apply those laws to that specific situation.

No book can take the place of sound legal advice. If the specific facts are not known, the applicable law cannot be identified and the likely outcome cannot be predicted. You'll learn more about this in Chapter 3, but for now understand that the best any author can do is introduce basic concepts in a general way, along with explanatory examples, and make readers aware of potential risks. Only you can know your tolerance for risk and only you can determine whether you need to seek legal advice, because only you can know the full context in which your problem exists.

Lawyers Must Be Licensed

Lawyers are licensed by the state. A lawyer can practice law only in states in which he holds a license and only when that license is in good standing with the state licensing authorities. A lawyer who disregards this rule and provides legal advice without a license (the "unauthorized practice of law") may permanently lose his license. That's a pretty harsh reality after successfully managing all of the hurdles to obtain the license in the first place.

State Laws Differ

State laws differ—sometimes wildly and sometimes just a bit. You will learn in the chapters that follow that while contract law, the practice, has remained relatively constant over the years, there are important nuances in the application of various states' laws that must be considered. A lawyer is expected to remain current with the developments in the areas of law in which he practices. It is malpractice to give legal advice about matters with which the lawyer is unfamiliar or not current.

Free or Low-Cost Legal Help

Many state and local (county or city) bar associations have free or low-cost walk-in clinics or referral services, so give that a try if you are too nervous to handle the problem on your own. If your issue concerns a contract, bring it and any supporting paperwork with you. When I volunteered at legal clinics in New York City, I can't tell you how many times someone walked in the door seeking advice—often regarding an apartment lease or a performing contract—without the contract in hand. A guessing game is of no value to anyone.

Chapter 9 provides some guidance for those looking for legal clinics and attorney referrals. It also provides suggestions for online self-help resources and a listing of some helpful books with my annotations.

HOW TO USE THIS BOOK

If you don't understand how contracts work, they can be daunting. Sometimes they seem drafted in a way to be intentionally confusing. But you can learn to understand them. Like anything worth doing, it just takes practice. I applaud you for diving in.

Use this book as a guidebook. It is not necessary that you read it cover to cover. If you do, you will gain a deeper understanding of contract basics because of the order in which the material is presented. But you don't have to. You can use it as a reference when you are confronted with unfamiliar language or when a specific question arises.

Here is a quick reference chart to point you in the right direction:

Issue	Where to Look
I need some free (or low-cost) legal help	Chapter 9
What's the difference between an agent and a manager?	Chapter 8
I don't understand my manager's contract	Chapters 5 and 8
I don't understand my gig contract	Chapters 5 and 7
My gig/manager's contract has clauses/language you don't discuss in Chapter 7 or 8	Chapter 5
I'm not sure if I have a "real" contract or not	Chapter 2
I have a contract and can't get paid	Chapters 3 and 9
How does contract law work?	Chapters 1 and 2

NEGOTIATION, NOT LITIGATION

This book is not intended to promote litigation. It can't be overemphasized that negotiation, not litigation, is the best way to proceed when a dispute arises. This isn't to say that you shouldn't be fully prepared to exercise all your rights, including litigation, and to demonstrate your ability to do so. But most contract disputes are settled through negotiation and mutual compromise, where both parties to a dispute are willing to be reasonable.

Lawsuits are costly and time-consuming. Additionally, litigation can tie up all kinds of resources that non-profits can't spare. The result of litigation will very likely be the loss of the business relationship. If that is of no consequence to you, then you ask yourself if it isn't better to just walk away from the relationship with wallet and reputation intact.

Negotiating through a dispute, where possible, will show you to be more businesslike and may preserve the relationship for future work. And the next time you will have much more knowledge of that party and their practices than you had before the dispute arose and will be in a better position to avoid the same issue in the future. Knowledge is power.

DO IT!

My hope for you is that you feel empowered to confidently manage all your financial decisions—personal and professional, contract or not. Too many graduates of arts programs feel overwhelmed by business and money matters and eventually throw in the towel. I hope that, with this book, you will begin to consider yourself a business—a business in which you are the CEO, and in which you and your craft, taken together, are a brand that you are developing and promoting. Good luck!

PART I

CONTRACT LAW AND THE AMERICAN LEGAL SYSTEM

A Brief Overview of the American Legal System

This chapter provides a brief overview of the American legal system and how contract law fits within that legal framework.

A COMMON LAW SYSTEM VERSUS A CIVIL LAW SYSTEM

With the notable exception of Louisiana, the United States inherited its system of law—the *common law* system—from England. Louisiana, being a former French territory, inherited its legal system from France. France follows a *civil law* system based on the Napoleonic Code. A legal system based on a "code" means that the laws are all organized in some way and written down. The *common law* system uses codes too (statutes), but the bulk of our "law" is found in court decisions. Nothing contained in this book is relevant to contracts governed by the laws of Louisiana.

THE ROLE OF HISTORY (PRECEDENT) IN THE COMMON LAW SYSTEM

Under a *common law* system, in addition to the local, state, and federal laws, there is a huge body of law resulting from court decisions. Although each decision theoretically affects only the parties to that case, reported decisions affect the overall body of law applicable to everyone because of a system of precedent called (in Latin) *stare decisis*; it requires that cases be decided based on precedent, or how previous cases with similar fact patterns were decided in the past. Under a *common law* system, facts are supreme. A lawyer arguing a case advocates on behalf of his client by drawing parallels and distinctions between the current case and previously decided cases based on his client's best interests. The importance of facts in a *common law* system cannot be overstated.

The term *civil law* can be confusing because, in addition to referring to an entire legal system as noted above, it is also a term used within our common law system to refer to an entire body of law: non-criminal law. The United States' *common law* system can be divided into two parts: (1) criminal law and (2) *civil law*.

Contract law is an area of civil law, which means that if you break the promises you made to someone under a contract—an act referred to as a *breach of contract*—it is generally not a crime. However, there are *remedies* available to the person you harmed by breaking your promise, and they usually involve money.

CONTRACT LAW

Contract law is not a "law," such as *you must wear a seat belt when driving an automobile*. Instead, it is a collection of laws and court decisions that, taken together, govern contracts.

Although there is similarity across state lines, every state has its own nuanced version of the laws governing who may contract and how. Where states differ is largely dependent on how previous contract disputes were settled in that jurisdiction and the reasoning used to get to those resolutions.

CONTRACTS AND SOCIETY

Contracts serve an important function in society because they bring a measure of certainty to an uncertain world. Contracts memorialize our promises to one another and spell out what will happen if we break those promises. This stabilizes business arrangements and reins in the transaction costs of doing business.

For these reasons, contracts permeate our society. Contract law governs formal, written agreements such as leases, mortgages, and car rental agreements as well as informal, quasi-written agreements like airline tickets and dry cleaner receipts. Contract law also governs non-written arrangements like hiring a babysitter or selling an old sofa online. These are all examples of some type of contract, and they are all as equally binding as the most complicated, formal witnessed and notarized contract.

In addition to promoting an orderly society, contracts are uniquely powerful tools because they can change the law that governs a deal between two parties. Often, contracts spell out what the law requires, but sometimes contracts change the law, temporarily, for a specific situation. For example, if the law provides a six-year statute of limitations to make a legal claim that someone broke a contractual promise, we can agree that for just our deal, the period for making a legal claim will be only two years. In doing this, we just changed the law that governs our arrangement.

Another common example is an Arbitration Clause (see Chapter 5), in which you can contractually agree to waive your right to a jury trial and resolve any future dispute via arbitration instead.

While contracts can be a powerful tool in commerce, that power is limited, as you will learn when you read about the contractual requirements of *validity* and *enforceability* in Chapter 2.

LEGAL VERSUS MORAL OBLIGATIONS

Contracts tell us what our legal obligations are to each other. While embedded in contract law is the requirement that we treat each other honestly, contracts dictate only legal obligations, not moral obligations.

This is an important distinction to understand. For example, if you asked me whether you have an obligation to report suspected child abuse to the authorities, my response would be, "What kind of obligation?" Hopefully, most would say that all members of society have a moral obligation to report suspected child abuse, but that obligation springs from a person's own moral code, not from a legal requirement.

The answer to whether one has a *legal* obligation is different. It depends on whether the law or a contract has imposed a legal obligation (referred to as a "duty"). In approximately forty-eight states, certain professions are designated as having a legal (statutory) duty to report suspected child abuse to the authorities.[1] Additionally, some employers might contractually require such reporting. So, based on the subject matter and profession, some people may owe a higher duty to others than what ordinary citizens may owe.

In the next chapter, we will look at contracts in detail, beginning with a definition of *contract*, and consider different types of contracts, the requirements of *validity* and *enforceability*, and what types of contracts *must* be in writing to be enforceable.

2

Contract Basics

So, what is a contract? Stated most simply, a contract is a promise (or set of promises) that society will enforce. Most contracts are of the "set of promises" variety, or *bilateral*. *Bilateral* contracts contain a set of promises where one party promises something for the other party's return promise. In the context of performers, it is often a scenario in which a presenter promises to pay an artist a certain amount of money at a certain time and the artist promises to perform at the presenter's venue on a certain date and for a certain time period.

In the much less common *unilateral* contract, the offering party makes a promise to the other party, but instead of seeking a promise in return (as is required in a *bilateral* contract), he seeks full (completed) performance instead. A reward for a lost dog is a good example of a *unilateral* contact: the dog's owner posts that she will pay $1,000 for the safe return of her dog. She is promising to pay, but will only pay for full performance (the safe return of her dog). She is not asking for any promise in exchange for her promise to pay. *Unilateral* contracts are rare and not the focus of this guidebook.

RIGHTS, DUTIES, AND RESTRICTIONS

The promises we make to one another under a contract can be broken down into rights and duties. Each party to a contract has certain duties they are promising to perform under the contract. For musicians, those duties usually require performing as a musician, though there may be other duties such as supplying their own instruments, arranging music, hiring others, etc. Conversely, a presenter's duties under a contract with musicians usually start with supplying the venue and paying the musicians.

Musicians' rights under a performing contract are usually to be paid for performing and anything else they've agreed to, such as to receive publicity for the event. The presenter's rights begin with having the musicians perform as contracted.

Both parties to the contract will also likely have certain restrictions apply to the relationship. These will vary by context, but usually these involve the restrictions against making *unilateral* changes to the contract (via an Amendment Clause), restrictions against substituting another musician to perform (via an Assignment Clause), and various other restrictions necessary to make the arrangement work.

WRITTEN VERSUS UNWRITTEN CONTRACTS

Do contracts have to be in writing? As with so many legal questions, the best answer is, "It depends." Not all contracts have to be in writing, but some contracts are required by law to be in writing in order to be *enforceable* and those will be discussed below; see *Statute of Frauds*.

But generally, written and non-written contracts are *valid* and *enforceable*. Non-written contracts are called *oral contracts*. When it comes to law, semantics are very important because some words are considered terms of art and, as such, hold a special meaning that is more specific than their colloquial meaning. *Oral contract* is a term of art. There is no such thing as a *verbal* contract. As long as a verbal agreement contains all of the required elements of a contract, it is a *valid oral contract*. *Oral contracts* are just as valid and hold the same weight as written contracts, but for the obvious reason that the actual terms of an *oral contract* are not in a signed writing, they can be harder to prove and enforce.

WHO CAN CONTRACT

Individual states determine who may contract. Generally, the only requirements are that the person be of a minimum age and possess the mental competence to understand the nature of what she is doing. A child, such as a child star, can have a guardian, such as a parent, contract on her behalf, but states will often look out for the child's interests by requiring that those contracts be reviewed and approved by an independent, court-appointed lawyer.

VALIDITY

The focus of this guidebook will be the analysis and interpretation of the most common type of contracts: written, *bilateral* contracts. Examples of these are apartment leases, mortgages, credit card agreements, rental car agreements, and, of course, performers' contracts. Contracts for the sale of goods are outside the scope of this guidebook.

There are four required elements in a *valid bilateral* contract. Using the mnemonic device CODA, they are:

C—consideration

O—offer

D—definite terms

A—acceptance

There must be an offer and acceptance of definite terms, supported by consideration.

Offer and Acceptance

Let's start with the O and A. The O stands for *offer*, the A for *acceptance* of that offer.

Referred to as *mutuality*, offer and acceptance, taken together, are the skeletal framework on which the entire contract, as a construct, depends. *Mutuality*, or the evidencing of mutual assent, is the assumption that a deal was freely negotiated, unencumbered by duress and undue influence, and that a true meeting of the minds took place, resulting in both parties' desire to enter into an arrangement evidencing an intent to be legally bound to each other under a contract.

It is important to point out that *mutual assent*, in this context, is not the subjective intent of each of the parties, but rather the objective intent—one that a reasonable person would conclude based on the facts. The *mutuality* requirement is so important that it is common to see it referenced in a preamble at the top of a contract (". . . thus the parties mutually agree as follows: . . .").

This preamble language is referred to as the *Mutuality Provision*. Lack of such language will not invalidate a contract, but including it is an indication to anyone interpreting the contract that the drafter is intending to make clear that *mutual assent* is important and, in fact, exists as the basis for the agreement.

Offers

Offers are not open forever. If no time period for acceptance is stated in the offer, then a "reasonable period of time" will be interpreted by a court for the offer's natural expiration.

An offer can end by:

1. being revoked by the offeror (except for offers that are expressly stated to be irrevocable);
2. being expressly rejected by the offeree (the person to whom the offer was made);
3. the offeree making a counter offer to the offeror; or
4. operation of law, which means:
   i.   after a "reasonable period of time";
   ii. if the offer spells out an expiration date; or
   iii. if performance under the contract becomes impossible (the offeror dies or becomes mentally incompetent; the subject matter of the offer is destroyed—particularly when involving the sale of goods or real estate; or the contract becomes illegal in some way (e.g., the law changes).

Acceptance

There are two important things to keep in mind with *acceptance*:

1. The offeror controls the means of acceptance. To accept an offer, you must accept it according to the terms that the offer may require, if any. For example, if the offer states that you must call the offeror by noon on Friday to accept it, then emailing her by 12:45 p.m. on Friday does not, technically, constitute acceptance. Under this scenario, if a dispute arises later and you attempt to enforce the contract, the offeror can raise a *validity defense* by correctly pointing out that no contract existed because you didn't comply with the offer's terms of acceptance. Whether that would actually work depends on what transpired between you two in the interim.

2. Changing the terms of an offer = rejecting the offer. To accept an offer, you must accept all its terms without conditions or limitations. For example, if a presenter offers you a gig to perform two 50-minute sets of music in a two-hour period, but you write back and say that you only want to perform two 40-minute sets, you have rejected the offer and created a counter offer. In this scenario, the offer made to you is now dead; you killed it with your counter offer. It cannot be revived by your later saying, "OK, I've changed my mind. I will do two 50-minute sets." You would now have to wait and see if the presenter accepts your counter offer.

Additionally, if you receive an offer via contract and you cross things out, initialing your changes, you are killing the offer and creating a counter offer.

Contract Acceptance and Signing

Traditional contract signings are not required to be witnessed or notarized unless the contract itself calls for such formalities. The reason for requiring witnesses and/or notarization is to have proof that a signature belongs to the party who is trying to deny that it is his.

D Stands for *Definite Terms*

What are *definite terms*? Great question! Who knows for sure? Essentially, *definite terms* are those terms necessary for the contract to be performed. What is definite and necessary will depend on the context. Contracts should spell out the names of the parties, subject matter of the contract, dates, and monetary details. A performer's contract may also include information regarding location of performance(s) and rehearsal(s); role or part; language, if relevant; who receives payment, performer or manager, and when; any per diem amount; and housing allowance and travel arrangement information, if relevant.

See Chapter 7 for the elements commonly required in *personal services contracts* and for an annotated *presenter's engagement contract*. See Chapter 8 for clauses commonly found in an *artist-management contract*. Those chapters will provide guidance for understanding what constitutes definite terms for performers' contracts. What is definite will depend on context.

Contracts can fail for lack of specificity of key (*definite*) terms because if each party had a different interpretation or understanding of one or more of the key elements of a contract, then there would not be a true meeting of the minds and the contract would fail (be invalid) for lack of *mutuality*.

EXAMPLE 2.1

IMPROPER ACCEPTANCE OF OFFER

A conductor has assembled a small orchestra to perform her own compositions in a public performance next month. She calls Joe on Friday afternoon and makes the following offer: "I will pay you $500 if you will play in my orchestra on May 1, provided you call me by noon on Monday to accept."

The table provides various scenarios with the same result: no contract was formed because the offer was not properly accepted.

	Offeree's Response to Conductor's Offer	Result	Reasoning
1	Offeree (Joe) does nothing; next day Offeror (the conductor) calls to say she found someone else.	No contract was formed.	In communicating that she gave the gig to someone else, the Offeror (the conductor) revoked her offer before Joe could accept it.
2	Joe says, "I'm sorry, but I can't take the gig. I will be out of town that weekend."	No contract was formed.	The offer was rejected by Joe.
3	Joe says, "I will do the gig for $750."	No contract was formed.	By stating his willingness to take the gig for $750, Joe killed the $500 offer and created a counter offer. In doing so, he is precluded from backpedaling and saying yes to the original offer to play for $500; that offer is dead.
4	Joe does nothing and a few months pass with no communication between the conductor and Joe.	No contract was formed.	After a "reasonable period of time," offers expire by operation of law.
5	Joe responds to accept the gig on Monday evening.	No contract was formed.	Joe did not accept the offer according to the offer's stated terms; he responded too late.
6	Joe takes time to think over the offer; when he calls to accept the gig, he is told that the conductor passed away the night before.	No contract was formed.	When the conductor died, the offer died with her by operation of law because of the impossibility of her being able to conduct her own concert.

EXAMPLE 2.2

CONTRACT THAT FAILED FOR LACK OF MUTUALITY

There is a famous old case involving parties who entered into an agreement to ship goods on a ship called *Peerless*. However, there were actually two ships with that name, and they had different sailing and arrival dates. Because it was determined that the parties had differing understandings regarding the ship and its sailing and arrival dates, the deal failed because the contract was judged invalid for lack of mutuality. No contract means that the party suing the other for breach of contract was simply out of luck, so he could not get monetary damages for his loss/inconvenience.

C Stands for *Consideration*

Finally, the *C* stands for *consideration*. *Consideration* is defined as a "bargained-for exchange of values"—often, money for an act, but not always. A promise from one person that induces the promise of another has been deemed valid *consideration* under a *bilateral* contract—much like a barter situation.

Refraining from exercising a legal right to which one is entitled is also valid *consideration*. For example, if you agree to release someone from a debt he owes you in exchange for the other person to wash your car every Saturday for the next six weeks, your agreement to not pursue the debt is valid *consideration* in support of the car washing deal. However, it is not valid *consideration* to refrain from telling the world a secret in exchange for money because that is illegal (extortion).

Courts generally will not get involved in determining whether *consideration* is adequate, particularly the amount of payment for some service provided. But they will step in if a deal is premised on nominal (pretend) *consideration*. A deal unsupported by valid *consideration* is deemed merely to be a promise to make a gift. Promises to make a gift are *unenforceable* for lack of *consideration*, but there are some notable exceptions in the world of philanthropy and non-profit institutions.

No *consideration* = a promise to make a gift.

EXAMPLE 2.3

CONTRACT THAT FAILED FOR LACK OF CONSIDERATION

Having always been fond of Kyle's daughter, Ali, Joe promises Kyle to have his band play at Ali's Sweet Sixteen party but doesn't follow through with it. Kyle has no recourse against Joe because the promise to play was not supported by consideration. This was a promise to make a gift and, as such, Kyle has no recourse against Joe when Joe doesn't follow through on his promise.

Recall the story about my friend, the director, from the preface. He was able to collect his fee when the opera company canceled his production because he had a *valid* contract, wherein he agreed to direct an opera in exchange for the opera company paying him a fee.

The *consideration*, in that case, was found in his commitment to direct the production: he cleared his schedule and held those dates for the opera company. The opera company had no defensible position to say that no *valid* contract was formed because their agreement met the four CODA elements: (1) they made the offer to hire him; (2) he accepted that offer as presented; (3) the terms were definite (which production, where, when, how long, for how much compensation); and (4) it was supported by consideration (he cleared his schedule and held those dates for them). Therefore, he was entitled to receive his fee because the opera company breached its agreement with him.

Illegal Contracts of Adhesion

You've learned that *consideration*, as the "bargained for exchange of values," is central to the *validity* of a contract because it makes a set of promises binding upon the parties to an agreement and distinguishes those promises from a promise to make a gift, which is not *enforceable*. The "bargaining" part of contract negotiation doesn't necessarily mean that there were days of back-and-forth, heated negotiating between the parties. It means that each party to the deal gave something up in exchange for the other's promise.

Often, however, the parties to a negotiation have grossly unequal bargaining power, resulting in a "take it or leave it" attitude from one side of the deal. In that instance, what kind of real bargaining is taking place? This is especially true in the case of creative people who are trying to get hired by a presenting organization, whether it's an opera company, orchestra, art gallery, or theater.

Historically, "take it or leave it" contract "negotiating" has been carefully considered by courts, resulting in the term *contracts of adhesion*; such contracts are illegal. A *contract of adhesion* is one in which the parties to a contract have unequal bargaining power such that there is no real negotiating taking place *and* the contract contains terms that are unconscionable (extremely unjust). This two-prong test regarding what constitutes a *contract of adhesion* may be the same in many, if not all, states, but the underlying legal test to determine the individual elements—in this case, what is unconscionable—often differ. There are often critical nuances embedded in the underlying legal tests that are a result of the different facts from actual contract disputes resolved in those jurisdictions. What is unconscionable in one state or region may be different from another based on unique histories.

So, not all contracts resulting from grossly unequal bargaining power are illegal. The second part of the test is most important: Are the *terms* of the contract unconscionable based on precedent in that jurisdiction? This inquiry would be done by a fact-finder—usually a judge or jury.

Illusory Promises and Aleatory Promises

Another promise that will fall short of being a contract is an illusory promise. An illusory promise is one in which one party has made no true commitment to the other party. Where there is no true commitment, nothing given up for the other's promise, there is no exchange of *consideration*. Illusory promises don't rise to the level of being a contract because one party does not have any real obligation to the other.

EXAMPLE 2.4

ILLUSORY PROMISES

a. "I might buy your car if you advertise it for sale this week for under $7,500."

b. "If you can polish up the Goldberg Variations by summer, I may hire you to play at my festival."

In Example 2.4, neither of the speakers commits to doing anything, so no contract is formed.

Distinct from an illusory promise, however, is an aleatory promise. An aleatory promise is one in which one party's performance under the contract is conditioned upon some future event taking place that is wholly outside of the control of that promisor.

EXAMPLE 2.5

ALEATORY PROMISES

a. "I will pay you $500 if your son scores 75 or more points in tonight's basketball game."

b. "I will engage you as a soloist in my *Messiah* this December if the church makes time in its calendar for it."

Other common examples are mortgage contingency clauses in real estate sales contracts and employment offers by law firms to law students if the students pass the bar exam.

Aleatory promises are valid; illusory promises are not.

ENFORCEABILITY

Now you know the four required (CODA) elements for a *valid* contract, but *validity* is only the first inquiry when trying to determine whether, and the extent to which, contractual rights exist. The second inquiry is *enforceability*—in other words: Can I enforce the rights that I have under this *valid* contract? For a *valid* contract to be *enforceable*, it must not: (1) be against *public policy*; or (2) violate the *Statute of Frauds*.

Public Policy

Citing *public policy* to render a contract *unenforceable* has been said to be a means of last resort and is called upon only when neither the facts nor the law are on your side. What is against *public policy* is difficult to determine because it is an idea largely shaped by culture. Criminal activity is against *public policy*. A person could sign a contract that meets the CODA criteria for *validity*, but the subject matter of the contract could, nonetheless, render it *unenforceable*. A contract for murder or a contract between a pharmacist and a physician to illegally distribute controlled narcotics are examples of *unenforceable* contracts because these are criminal acts and, therefore, against *public policy*. In California, for example, *personal services contracts* with a duration beyond seven years are against *public policy* and, therefore, *unenforceable*.

Famous Public Policy Case

Many years ago, the United States Supreme Court heard a case involving a legal challenge to a restrictive covenant[1] in the bylaws of a homeowners' association. In that case, a homeowner was challenged by his association for selling his home to a member of a minority class, because doing so violated a clause in the association's bylaws. Because homeowners' association bylaws are contracts, they are very difficult, if not impossible, to dismantle. Notably, in this case, the court held that while the bylaws met the requirements of *validity* as a binding contract between its members and the association, the restriction against transferring property to minorities was struck down as being against *public policy*—and allowing it to stand based solely on principles of contract construction would establish an untenable precedent.

Another *public policy* example, involving building contractors, is discussed in *Contracts: The Essential Business Desk Reference.*[2] There, the author points out that courts often find that contracts offered by unlicensed contractors, such as home improvement guys, are *unenforceable* because to allow them to stand would undermine the policy of the licensing laws. In other words, even if those contracts are *valid*, they are *unenforceable* because they are against *public policy.*

Statute of Frauds

Easier to grasp than the concept of *public policy* is the *Statute of Frauds*, which was enacted in England in 1677. It holds that while not all contracts need to be in writing, some are so important that they are required to be in writing (or some form of a writing) to be *enforceable*. Most states, if not all of them, have enacted some version of the original *Statute of Frauds*, but while there are some common elements across state lines, they are likely not entirely uniform.

One element of the *Statute of Frauds* is an important one for performers to know about: any contract that, on its face, cannot be fully performed within a year of its making must be in writing to be *enforceable*. Musicians are often asked to book gigs far in advance of the performance date, so it is important to understand that if the performance date is more than a year away from the date of the handshake, you will need the deal reduced to some form of a writing for it to be enforceable as a contract. In other words, if it's not in writing, you will not have any grounds to assert that you have an *enforceable oral contract* because the gig is more than a year away from the date you verbally accepted it.

As an example, New York State's *Statute of Frauds* is encoded within New York's General Obligations Law. The pertinent part to illustrate this concept is:

EXAMPLE 2.6

§5-701. AGREEMENTS REQUIRED TO BE IN WRITING

Every agreement, promise or undertaking is void, unless it or some note or memorandum thereof be in writing, and subscribed by the party to be charged therewith, or his lawful agent, if such agreement, promise or undertaking: (1) by its terms is not to be performed within one year from the making thereof . . .

The "memorandum" of a writing referenced in Example 2.6 refers to the idea that different pieces of written information (like an e-mail and other notes) can constitute a "writing" for the purposes of satisfying the *Statute of Frauds* in New York when considered as a whole. I think it can be inferred that the New York State Assembly, when enacting its version of the *Statute of Frauds*, recognized that people don't always reduce their contractual relationships to a formal writing and that sometimes the best we have are bits and pieces of written communication that can function as a contract when considered as a whole. In other words, if this is all you have to support the idea that a contractual relationship was intended, then you get the benefit of the doubt.

"Subscribed by the party to be charged" means signed by the party against whom enforcement is sought. In other words, if you need to enforce a contract that cannot be fully performed within a year of entering into the contract, the other person must have signed something in order for you to have rights to enforce. This is much less of an issue today because an email constitutes a "signing." Of course, it works both ways: if you try to back out of such a contract, it can be enforced against you, but only if you've signed it. The term *agent*, as used within Example 2.6, refers to agents *generally*, not a licensed theatrical agent or an artist manager.

See Chapter 8 for a discussion of licensed theatrical agents. See Chapter 9 for a hypothetical situation involving an oral contract.

3

Breach of Contract (When Things Go Wrong)

In the real-life example provided in the preface, my director friend promised to direct an opera and the opera company promised to pay him for his time and talent. When the opera company contacted him in advance of his scheduled arrival date to tell him that they were canceling his production, they were telling him that they were going to break their promise to him. This is called an *anticipatory breach of contract*.

In the material that follows in this chapter you'll learn that:

- the director and the opera company had *privity of contract*;
- paying his fee was *material* (a substantial part of the agreement made between the director and the opera company);
- when they told him they would be breaking their promise to him, he was entitled to a *remedy* (to receive the fee they promised him); and
- he was required to *mitigate* his *damages*, if possible.

When one party is accused of not following through with his commitments pursuant to a contract, it's referred to as a *breach of contract*. Contracts often, but not always, contain language that spells out what options (or *remedies*) are available to the non-breaching party as a consequence of the other party's *breach*, but usually the non-breaching party wants one of two things, depending on her position at the time of the *breach*: (1) to force the contract according to its terms, or (2) money (referred to as *damages*).

Because contract law is governed by state law, each state determines, by statute, what the statute of limitations is for bringing a *breach of contract* action against the breaching party. For example, in New York the statute of limitations is six years for bringing a *breach of contract* legal action against someone for breaking their contractual promises to you. Chapter 9 provides guidance for determining what the statutes of limitations are in other states.

PRIVITY

Privity is an old word representing an old idea: it stands for the principle that parties to a contract have a special relationship that arises out of their obligations to one another and, as such, only they are entitled to claim that a *breach* has taken place and only they have rights to enforce under the contract. This was the old *common law* rule resulting from past court decisions, but today it has been relaxed some recognizing that we live in a more complex world.

Today, certain people by their status as *intended third-party beneficiaries* under other parties' contracts can sue to enforce the rights given to them under contracts in which they have not actively taken part.

Third-party beneficiaries are just that: they are people or entities who would benefit as the result of other parties entering into a contract, but only *intended third-party beneficiaries* have rights under a contract to which they are not a party. People or entities who would coincidentally benefit from others' contractual promises are called *incidental third-party beneficiaries* and, as such, have no rights to enforce when one of those other parties breaks their contractual promises to the other.

Continuing with the story of the opera director, only he had *privity* of contract with the opera company, so only he could sue it for *breach of contract* if it came to that.

So, if he owed his neighbor money and told him that he would repay him after he directed the opera production and received his fee, the neighbor would have no standing to assert a *breach of contract* claim against the opera company because the neighbor and the opera company lack *privity*. In this scenario, the neighbor is an *incidental third-party beneficiary* to that contract.

On the other hand, if both the director and the opera company *intended* to make the neighbor a beneficiary of the opera production contract, then the neighbor would have standing to sue the company for *breach of contract* when it cancelled.

EXAMPLE 3.1

LACK OF PRIVITY AS AN INCIDENTAL THIRD-PARTY BENEFICIARY

Ali, a singer-songwriter, contracts to perform at a restaurant for several nights for a total of $500. Ali also owes me $500. She tells me that she will repay me once she is paid for her restaurant gig.

If the restaurant cancels her gig, I have no standing to exert any rights against the restaurant because I am not an intended third-party beneficiary of Ali's contract with the restaurant. In this example, I am an *incidental* third-party beneficiary to Ali's contract with the restaurant; therefore, I have no viable claim against it for breach of contract. Ali, of course, would have a breach of contract claim against the restaurant provided that all of the required elements for validity exist.

In addition to having *privity of contract*, a party claiming that a *breach* has occurred must demonstrate that the *breach* was *material*. A *material breach* by one party to a contract will excuse performance by the other party.

MATERIALITY

The failure to do something inconsequential under a contract will not necessarily amount to a *breach*. For an act or a failure to act under a contract to amount to a *breach*, it must be important enough to frustrate the essential purpose of contracting in the first place. This is known as *materiality*; in others words, not inconsequential.

Some contract drafters will indicate, in the contract itself, what constitutes a *material breach* under the contract, but this is rare. Doing so puts the other party on notice that if that specific promise is not met, it will result in a substantial problem for the other party that will be considered by him to be a *material breach* to the extent that it will frustrate the entire purpose of the contract.

EXAMPLE 3.2

MATERIALITY CLAUSE

Failure of Artist to be off-book and have a reasonable working-knowledge of the Russian libretto pursuant to items 6(a) through (d), above, shall constitute a material breach of this Engagement Agreement.

Most contracts don't contain Materiality Clauses. One way to determine whether an act (or failure to act) under a contract could be *material* is to consider whether one of the duties owed, by you to another or to you by another, is at issue. In other words, if the contract requires you to perform (your duty) and you did not, that would likely be *material* and could serve as the basis for a *breach of contract* action against you. Similarly, if you are a musician who performed and can't get paid, the other party to your engagement contract is likely in *breach* of the contract because paying someone is a duty in a *personal services contract* and the failure to pay is a *material* element of that contract.

In the absence of a Materiality Clause, courts will consider whether or not the breaching party *substantially* performed his contractual promises. In other words, did the breach that took place rise to the level of being *material*, such that the overall purpose of the contract was frustrated?

Generally, courts consider the following:

- the ability of the non-breaching party to be compensated for his loss caused by the *breach*
- whether the breaching party acted in bad faith
- the extent to which the breaching party could rectify the situation
- how far into the contract the parties were at the time the breach occurred/ whether the non-breaching party was notified of an *anticipatory breach*
- whether the non-breaching party was ready to perform his contractual promises
- the extent to which the non-breaching party got what he contracted for

Once a *breach* has taken place, the non-breaching party cannot sit back and allow his losses to grow, expecting to recoup them via legal means. The law requires him to *mitigate* (limit) his potential for loss arising out of the other party's *breach*.

THE DUTY TO MITIGATE DAMAGES

In a *breach of contract* action, the party who has not breached is entitled to *expectation damages* minus any expenses that she would have incurred if the contract were fully performed. However, the law imposes a legal duty for the non-breaching party to *mitigate* any *damages* that arise as a consequence of the *breach*.

EXAMPLE 3.3

MITIGATING DAMAGES

You contracted to perform at the Kennedy Center for $5,000, but the presenter canceled the performance two months before the engagement (an anticipatory breach). In this example, you are entitled to your $5,000 fee, but if you accept another opportunity during the originally contracted period for $3,000, you are legally entitled to only $2,000 in damages from the Kennedy Center presenter. If you accept both the $5,000 in damages and the $3,000 fee for the second gig, the presenter has the right to sue you for the $3,000 you collected but were not entitled to.

The example above illustrates the ethical proposition that a non-breaching party cannot unfairly benefit from another party's *breach*. The scenario described in Example 3.3 rarely occurs because the current practice in the arts is that when a presenter has to cancel an engagement contract with an artist, they usually just renegotiate a new arrangement for a future, possibly more valuable, engagement for that artist.

And, as discussed below in Remedies, if a performer cancels a concert, the presenter will not be able to legally force her to go through with the performance (the equitable remédy of *specific performance*), but he can obtain another form of *equitable relief*—an injunction to prevent her from performing elsewhere. But this *remedy* is so distasteful and would be so widely criticized, it is hard to image that it would be utilized today.

Going back to the story of the opera director from the preface, getting paid for performing a service is *material*. It is a fundamental purpose for contracting. Once the director was notified that the production would not be taking place, he had a duty to *mitigate* his *damages*. This means he had a legal duty to accept similar work during that same time period, if possible, and was precluded from making his financial position worse by spending money on items needed specifically for the canceled production (for example, renting a hotel room to stay in since he already had purchased airfare to that city).

If you recall from the beginning of the director's story, he called the opera company representatives and asked for his fee due to their cancellation and they tried to raise an objection. They didn't take the position that their *breach* was not *material*. Thinking that he would cut his losses and quietly go away, they said the contract's Force Majeure Clause excused their performance under the contract. You will learn about force majeure in Chapter 5, but essentially they were improperly raising the *contract defense* of *impossibility*, which, if successful, would excuse both his having to direct the opera and their having to pay him for doing it.

CONTRACT DEFENSES

Everyone is familiar with the affirmative defense of *self-defense* to a murder charge. Similarly, there are several defenses available in a *breach of contract* action. Some of the defenses relate to the lack of *mutuality*. Recall the discussion of *mutuality* in Chapter 2. *Mutuality* is the concept of a meeting of the minds, where both parties make promises to each other and freely come to an agreement, intending to be contractually bound to the other.

The defenses relating to a lack of *mutuality* are: (1) *lack of capacity*, (2) *mutual mistake*, and (3) *duress*.

The Defense of Lack of Capacity

Lack of capacity means that the person asserting the defense lacked the requisite mental state to freely enter in to a contract and to be bound by her promises outlined in it. Examples of *lack of capacity* include not being of legal age to contract (no legal consent is available) or being mentally impaired in some way. Intoxication has been successfully raised as a *lack of capacity* defense.

EXAMPLE 3.4

LACK OF CAPACITY DEFENSE

A violinist, you strike up a conversation with a well-known (and noticeably intoxicated) conductor at a cocktail party who offers you a gig as a replacement for a soloist in an upcoming high-profile concert he will conduct. The conductor could assert a lack of capacity defense when you claim that an oral contract was formed from your conversation and was later breached by the conductor when he said he had no recollection of the conversation with you.

The Defense of Mutual Mistake

Mutual mistake also speaks to the lack of *mutuality*, because where both parties entered into a contract with differing understandings of the key subject matter of the contract, no true meeting of the minds took place. In addition to Example 3.5, see the real-life example of the ships named *Peerless* in Example 2.2.

EXAMPLE 3.5

MUTUAL MISTAKE DEFENSE

You sign a contract to organize a holiday flash mob musical event at Penn Station for rush hour on Christmas Eve. With 200 people well-rehearsed and in place at New York's Penn Station at the designated time, you learn that the other party was contracting for Newark's Penn Station, not New York's Penn Station. If you are sued for breach, you could raise mutual mistake as a defense because there was no true meeting of the minds; you and the other party had different locations in mind.

The Defense of Duress

The defense of *duress* speaks to a scenario where one party threatens (or perpetrates) violence against the other to coerce her into contracting. If one party signs a contract under *duress*, she is not exercising free will and therefore the *mutuality* requirement is not present.

EXAMPLE 3.6

DURESS DEFENSE

A presenter threatens to break the knuckles of a concert pianist if she doesn't sign a contract agreeing to perform a series of concerts celebrating a political regime's public centennial concert. If the pianist subsequently refuses to perform and is later sued for breach, she can raise duress as a breach of contract defense.

ADDITIONAL DEFENSES

Other defenses are (1) *impossibility*, (2) *illegality*, (3) *undue influence*, (4) *misrepresentation*, and (5) *unconscionability* (contracts of adhesion).

The Defense of Impossibility

Similar to the idea discussed in Chapter 2, where offers expire by operation of law if performance under the contract becomes impossible, the defense of *impossibility* is available to a party against whom a *breach of contract* is claimed if performing under the contract becomes impossible.

EXAMPLE 3.7

IMPOSSIBILITY DEFENSE

A composer, you have a contract to collaborate on a commissioned piece of music with a specific artist who dies before work on the piece has begun. The defense of impossibility can be raised if you are sued by the artist's estate for breach of contract, because it's not possible to collaborate with a deceased person on anything.

The Defense of Illegality

Similar to the illegality concept raised under the discussion of *public policy*, contracts involving illegal activities, even if they meet the four required CODA elements of validity, are still *unenforceable* because they are illegal. A contract to burn down a business so the owner can collect insurance money would be *unenforceable* due to *illegality*.

EXAMPLE 3.8

ILLEGALITY DEFENSE

You contract with a composer to play his trumpet concerto, *Atop the Brooklyn Bridge*, from the top of one of the support structures of the Brooklyn Bridge on Memorial Day. The illegality defense would be available because it is illegal (trespassing) to climb to the top of the bridge pylons.

However, where parties contract to do something legal, but which later becomes illegal for some reason, the *defense of impossibility*, not *illegality*, can be raised by the defendant being sued for *breach*.

EXAMPLE 3.9

IMPOSSIBILITY DEFENSE
(DUE TO LAW CHANGE)

You contract with a composer to play his trumpet concerto, *Atop the Brooklyn Bridge*, on that bridge's walkway, but two months later a zoning ordinance is passed that prohibits public performances anywhere on the bridge. If the composer sued you for breach, you could raise the defense of impossibility.

The Defense of Undue Influence

Rather than involving violence or threats as the *duress defense* requires, the *undue influence defense* arises when one party to a contract exploits his personal relationship with the other party by using excessive pressure to influence the other to contract and the contract unfairly benefits the influencing party.

EXAMPLE 3.10

UNDUE INFLUENCE DEFENSE

Your longtime voice teacher pressures you to sign a contract hiring her as your artist manager, and the contract gives her 50% of your annual gross earnings from whatever source for the next ten years.

The Defense of Misrepresentation

The *misrepresentation defense* involves the use of false or fraudulent statements to induce the other party to enter into a contract.

EXAMPLE 3.11

MISREPRESENTATION DEFENSE

You sign a contract with someone who represents himself as a seasoned artist manager with several high-profile clients, but later you learn that he is a complete fraud with a fake website and no appreciable experience in artist management. If he sues you for breach of contract, you could raise the defense of misrepresentation.

A *contract defense* is raised by a defendant (the party being sued) when he is sued for *breach of contract*. If his defense is unsuccessful, he will lose the lawsuit and be liable to the other party. Generally, in a *breach of contract* action, he will be liable for *damages*. *Damages*, one type of legal *remedy*, are a monetary award. In the following section, you will learn that there are two basic categories of *remedies*.

REMEDIES

As noted immediately above, *remedies* refers to the options available to the non-breaching party as a consequence of the other party's broken promises. Sometimes the contract language says, "If one of us doesn't do what we agreed to do under this contract, then the other person has a right to *X*." But spelling out what *remedies* are available is not required in the contract. The law will provide them to prevent injustice and compensate the non-breaching party for a *material breach*.

Remedies can be divided into two main types: (1) *remedies at law*, and (2) *equitable remedies*.

Remedies at Law

Remedies at law refers to monetary awards (which come in several varieties), but basic contract *damages* are called *expectation damages*. *Expectation damages* put the non-breaching party in the monetary position she would be in if no breach took place and the contract was fully performed as agreed.

Equitable Remedies

Equitable remedies are not monetary, but instead result when the non-breaching party asks the court to flex its muscle by ordering that someone do something or someone refrain from doing something. The types of *equitable remedies* most people are familiar with are restraining orders (such as those against stalkers) and injunctions.

While I was preparing this book, the pop singer Kesha (Kesha Rose Sebert) unsuccessfully sought an injunction in a New York City court against her producer, Lukasz Gottwald, known as Dr. Luke. Essentially, Kesha, through her attorney, asked the court to allow her to disregard her exclusive recording contract with Dr. Luke so she could record music with someone else (she alleged that he had sexually assaulted her years earlier and that she suffered from years of ongoing abuse). Injunctions are notoriously difficult to get because those seeking them usually need to prove that if the injunction is not granted, they will suffer irreparable harm.

New York Supreme Court Justice Shirley Kornreich wrote, "My instinct is to do the commercially reasonable thing . . . I don't understand why I have to take the extraordinary measure of granting an injunction." This case illustrates how seriously courts take contractual obligations.

One important equitable remedy concept that you may see in the context of a performer's contract is *specific performance.*

Specific Performance

Specific performance refers to the equitable remedy where the non-breaching party asks the court to step in and force the contract to be performed as written. The non-breaching party is essentially asking the court to force the deal. The remedy of *specific performance* is available only when a *remedy at law* (monetary damages) would not sufficiently compensate the non-breaching party for his loss.

Specific performance is very rarely available in professional services contracts (the variety of contracts that includes performers' contracts). Even if the court could force a breaching party to perform, it cannot guarantee that the performance would be carried out in good faith.

There is an old but famous case that demonstrates this principle. It involved an opera singer who had a contract to sing at a restaurant, but then told the owner that she was not going to perform because she got a better-paying gig with another restaurant. The first owner sued the singer for *breach of contract*, asking the court for *specific performance* ("Make her sing!"). The court said it couldn't do that; however, it said that it would provide the owner with an *equitable remedy*: an injunction. The court told the singer that she didn't have to sing for the first owner, but also said that she could not perform for the second owner (or anyone else) during that time period either. The *equitable remedy* of injunction was used to keep the singer from performing elsewhere. The court came to this solution because it knew if she were forced to perform as contracted, it would not be possible to control the quality of her performance; she might decide to not perform in good faith.

The moral of this story is if you need to cancel a gig, ask for permission to renegotiate the contract or ask for a release (in legal language, a *novation*) from the contract.

For one example of how the term *specific performance* may appear in a performer's contract, see Example 5.41.

PART II

THE NUTS AND BOLTS OF CONTRACT INTERPRETATION

4

Interpreting Contract Language: Eight Tips for Getting Started

Parsing through even layman-friendly contracts can be daunting, but business-to-business contracts (such as performers' contracts) can be especially difficult to understand due, in large part, to the lack of consumer-friendly drafting requirements resulting in the use of archaic jargon and unnecessary legalese. Years ago, there was a consumer protection movement that resulted in legislation requiring companies who use contracts as part of their interactions with non-business consumers to use "plain language"; ordinary citizens otherwise couldn't understand what they were agreeing to in their contracts with businesses. Signing your name and binding yourself to a contract whose terms you don't fully understand is clearly not a good idea. Plain language rules require using *you* and *our* in place of words like *obligor* and *oblige*. The rules also require using short, easy-to-understand sentences in the subject-verb, active voice format.

While the modern approach to contract writing in the context of consumer goods and services is to use plain English, it is not universally used in business-to-business contracts such as the ones performers are asked to sign. Being able to parse language is a skill that can be developed with practice. In time, you will be able to shut out the noise and see what's really going on.

OUTDATED HISTORICAL NECESSITY

I hereby promise and covenant to cease and desist my lewd and lascivious conduct henceforth.

It's not uncommon to see synonyms (or near synonyms) in legal documents. Language like that used in the example immediately above may exist for historical reasons or may be the result of an unskilled drafter trying to make a document sound "legal."

There was a time when modern English was still evolving. In England, after the Norman Conquest, legal documents in English had to be clear for all readers, including those who were used to important documents being in French, Latin, or Anglo-Saxon English. In order to make this possible, multiple words were used to convey the same meaning.

This practice continues today: if you post copyrighted material to YouTube without the copyright holder's permission to use her content, you may receive a cease and desist letter from the copyright owner's attorney. That attorney, even if she fully embraces plain language drafting rules, more than likely will not title her letter a "stop doing that" letter, because if she did, she would run the risk of your thinking that the letter is something *other than* a cease and desist directive. Sidestepping legal tradition makes attorneys nervous, so absent legislative directives, drafting practices evolve slowly.

The ancient necessity of wordiness has regrettably continued for this reason and because people like me who draft contracts for a living find it much easier to modify an existing document than to draft something from scratch.

THE CHOICE OF ACTIVE VERSUS PASSIVE VOICE

The modern trend taught in law schools is for contract drafters to use plain language, refrain from using archaic jargon where simpler terms will suffice, avoid unnecessarily long sentences, and use the active voice. However, sometimes writers choose to use the passive voice when they want to obscure who the actor is in the sentence. For example: "It was determined that allowing the property to go into foreclosure would result in the most favorable outcome." The reader of this sentence doesn't know *who* actually made that determination.

LEGALESE, AMBIGUITY, AND THE CONTRACT DRAFTER'S BURDEN

Unskilled drafters sometimes try to make their contracts sound more formal by using unnecessarily long or highly stylized words, but all this does is muddy the meaning. On the other hand, some words are *terms of art* and mean something very specific, so they must be used for that purpose, or the drafter risks another interpretation. For example, the term *oral contract* means a valid, unwritten contract, but *verbal contract* has no legal significance.

Unclear language can be fatal to a contract drafter's intent because it goes against a basic tenet of legal writing called *contra proferentem*. *Contra proferentem* loosely translates to "against the offeror/drafter." The idea being that if a contract contains a clause that is ambiguous on its face, the party who drafted it should bear the burden of risk because, as drafter, he was in the best position to make his intentions clear. So, under the doctrine of *contra proferentem*, the side who drew up the contract will likely lose a challenge to the meaning of a clause that is judged to be ambiguous.

CONTRACT INTERPRETATION

Contract disputes often arise because of ambiguous contract language. In determining whether the language is ambiguous, judges often use the "four corners rule" of contract interpretation. This rule says to look at only what is actually contained within the four corners of the document to determine the parties' intent. Recall from Chapter 2 that the question of intent refers to the objective intent of the parties (that of a reasonable person), not what they say they were intending or thinking at the time they entered into the contract. For this reason alone, contracts can be long and complicated, but a skilled drafter can reduce complicated to clear even if the result goes from long to longer.

EIGHT TIPS FOR CONTRACT INTERPRETATION

Tip #1: Recitals

Classically trained musicians may see the term *recitals* and think special rules apply to solo performances. Not true! *Recitals*, in this context, are recitations that appear at the beginning of a contract. They can readily be identified by the "whereas" language used. Now considered old-fashioned, *recitals* do serve an important function in a contract: they provide some context and background for third-party readers like judges and arbitrators, providing insight into the business purpose of the contract.

EXAMPLE 4.1

WHEREAS Artist is an opera singer specializing in the vocal repertory of Richard Wagner.

WHEREAS Samantha Jones is Artist's Manager.

WHEREAS Presenter is a not-for-profit organization whose business is presenting live operatic performances to the public for a fee.

WHEREAS Artist is engaged to perform the role of Erda in Wagner's *Der Ring des Nibelungen* to be sung in German.

WHEREAS Presenter acknowledges that Ms. Jones is Artist's authorized agent for the purposes of contractually binding Artist to perform at Presenter's venue (Engagement).

WHEREAS the Engagement shall take place at 8 p.m. on June 15–22, 2016, in New York, New York.

In Example 4.1, the *recitals* provide valuable contextual information to third parties interpreting this contract. For example, if the artist were accused of *breaching* her contract because the director alleged that she couldn't successfully manage aerial silks and trapeze work in the production, the artist might point to the *recitals* as evidence that no traditional artist who contracts to sing Erda could reasonably be expected to be able to perform aerial work.

In other words, *not* being able to perform aerial work does not rise to the level of being *material* under this contract, so no *breach* took place. The outcome would likely be different if the contract required such work, the artist warranted that she had experience with it, and the artist agreed to do it in this production.

Tip #2: Words of Limitation or Breadth
Look for words and phrases that expand or limit your rights under the contract. Common words and phrases are *sole/solely*, *arising out of*, and *including, but not limited to*. Taken out of context they are neutral, but consider how they operate in a clause or sentence to see what's really going on.

EXAMPLE 4.2	
Sole/Solely	
Limiting for Artist	Manager shall have the sole right to approve use of Artist's image.
Benefits Artist	Presenter's sole remedy for breach hereunder shall be limited to ten percent (10%) of actual damages.

The phrase *arising out of* is a bit subtler. It is generally used to convey breadth by attempting to include any and all things that cannot be contemplated and listed out in the contract at the time of entering into it.

EXAMPLE 4.3	
Arising out of	
Limiting for Artist	Artist shall defend, indemnify and hold Presenter, its officers, employees and agents harmless from and against any and all liability, loss, expense (including reasonable attorney's fees) or claims for injury or damages arising out of the performance of this Agreement.
Benefits Artist	Presenter shall procure the clearances and rights associated with Artist's engagement hereunder and be solely responsible for paying the licensing costs arising out of Artist's appearance.

Similarly, *including, but not limited to* attempts to include a non-exhaustive list of similar things that is open to expansion later.

EXAMPLE 4.4	
Including, but not limited to	
Limiting for Artist	Presenter may seek reimbursement from Artist for the following fees including, but not limited to . . .
Benefits Artist	Manager's responsibility to Artist is to guide Artist's career including, but not limited to . . .

Tip #3: Bilateral versus Unilateral Clauses

Bilateral clauses are those that equally benefit both parties to the contract, whereas *unilateral* clauses provide broader rights to one party over another. *Unilateral* clauses are not always bad; they may make sense depending on the context of the deal. Your job is to: (1) recognize the distinction, and (2) determine how it affects your rights when you see unequal treatment in your contracts.

BILATERAL VERSION OF A
TERMINATION CLAUSE

Either actor or producer may terminate this contract by giving
the other party not less than four (4) weeks' prior written notice
of termination.

UNILATERAL VERSION OF THE SAME
TERMINATION CLAUSE

Producer may terminate this contract by giving actor not less
than four (4) weeks' prior written notice of termination.

In the *bilateral* version, both actor and producer can end the contractual
relationship with four weeks' written notice to the other party. In the *unilateral* version, only the producer can end the agreement with such notice. The
unilateral version is silent as to what the actor's rights are with respect to termination of the contractual relationship.

Tip #4: Obligatory versus Optional Language
If you've read Chapter 2, you already know that language is particularly important in contracts. So, while it may seem tedious, the distinction between
some words are important because they illustrate the difference between what
is optional and what is contractually required.

In Example 4.6, try using the substituted phrase to see if the concept makes
sense.

Though in contemporary verbal communications *will* and *shall* are used
almost interchangeably, keep in mind that language used in contracts is more
formal and, as you will see in Tip #7 (*defined terms*), a narrower, more specific
meaning is often intended.

EXAMPLE 4.6

Word	Substitute Phrase	Example
May	"is permitted to"	Artist may elect to set aside three (3) weeks per year for personal time.
Must	"is required to"	Artist must remit Manager's fee percentage by the fifth (5th) day of each month following the month in which Artist's fees are earned.
Will	"agrees (in the future) to"	Artist will forward all professional inquiries for Artist's professional services to Manager without undue delay.
Shall	"has a duty to" or "is obligated to"	Artist has entered into an exclusive arrangement with Manager. Artist shall not similarly engage another Manager to work on Artist's behalf.

Tip #5: Sentence Diagramming

Sometimes diagramming a run-on or otherwise complicated sentence is the only way to get at its true meaning. Don't be embarrassed about doing this; sometimes it's the only way. In law school we were encouraged to draw pictures in order to understand complicated concepts.

Example 4.7 is an excerpt of a utility contract among three parties: the city, the supplier, and the consumer/account holder. If you're not used to reading content like this, it can be intimidating. Don't give up; it just takes practice.

EXAMPLE 4.7

AUTOMATIC AGGREGATION

ELECTRICITY PURCHASE AND SALE TERMS AND CONDITIONS

The City of X ("City"), pursuant to the aggregation authority conferred upon it by referendum and ordinance, selected Super Duper Energy Systems ("Seller") to supply the aggregation, and entered into a Power Supply Agreement with Seller ("Program Agreement"). You, the account holder ("Buyer") for each eligible account at the service address referenced on the letter accompanying (the "Account(s)") this document, and Seller agree to the Electricity Purchase and Sale Terms and Conditions ("Agreement") as of January 1, 2015 ("Effective Date"). Seller and Buyer individually referred to as "Party" and collectively as "Parties."

The easiest way to untangle sentences like these are to put them in the active voice (subject-verb) format. Start by looking for the action (verbs), then look for the actors (subjects). Once you have the subjects and verbs, look for who or what was acted upon. Example 4.8 lays out the content from the original paragraph, Example 4.7.

		EXAMPLE 4.8
Subject (Who?)	Verb (Did What?)	Object (to What?)
City	selected	Seller to supply the aggregation
City (also)	entered into	a power supply agreement
Buyer and Seller	agree	to the terms and conditions in the (purchase and sales) agreement as of January 1, 2015.

Sometimes when we read long or complicated sentences, our brains allow us to jump over words that we recognize, but whose meaning may not be clear. When you read contract language, be sure that you understand every word. Circle any word you don't recognize or whose meaning is unclear within the context that it appears. It may be defined later within the contract or you may have to ask the other party to provide *their* definition of it. Don't rely on a dictionary definition, because that may not be what the other party intends. *Aggregation*, used in Examples 4.7 and 4.8, is a term you may decide to inquire about.

Having diagrammed the sentence, you now know what's going on: the city chose an electricity supplier and entered into a contract for it to supply me with electricity in accordance with terms contained in the agreement dated in January.

Tip #6: Clause Titles/Headings
Though discussed in Chapter 5, this concept is important enough to be included here because it underscores the need to read every clause to determine each one's function within the contract. Relying solely on the titles/headings given to a clause can not only be misleading, but will keep you from potentially important information that you will have unwittingly agreed to.

Example 4.9 is titled "Governing Law." If you only read the title of the clause, you would miss the fact that this is a bundled clause that does four distinct things. It contains: (1) a New York Choice of Law Clause, (2) a Merger Clause, (3) an Amendment Clause, and (4) a Waiver Clause.

This is a great, real-life example of the importance of reading and understanding every clause rather than relying on what the clause titles/headings say.

EXAMPLE 4.9

GOVERNING LAW

This agreement, construed, interpreted and governed pursuant to the laws of New York State (1), is a complete and accurate manifestation of the understandings between the parties (2). It cannot be changed orally and can only be amended, modified (3) or waived (4) in writing, signed by both parties.

Tip #7: Defined Terms

Some contracts, like insurance policies, have a formal Definitions section somewhere in the contract where terms are listed (usually alphabetically) and defined. It is critical to understand that whenever a term is defined in a contract, its meaning is being narrowed to something very specific. So, when you see a *defined term*, slow down and read the definition within the context of the sentence. You may even choose to first read the sentence without the *defined term* to see if that lends some clarity. Then read the definition and go back and reread the sentence, inserting the entire definition into it. Chapter 6 will give you a strategy for making this task easier.

EXAMPLE 4.10

Gross income means earnings, per diems, travel expenses, master class and other teaching fees and salaries, cash prizes, stocks, bonds, cash, sales, royalties, leases and bonuses.

Tip #8: Other Terms

If you see the term *condition precedent* used in a contract, it means that some condition must be met before some right arises.

EXAMPLE 4.11

As a condition precedent to admission into the Young Artist Development Program ("The Program"), Artist must have successfully completed her undergraduate studies and shall provide proof of graduation via official transcripts before Day 1 of orientation for The Program.

The phrase *incorporation by reference* within a contract means that there is another document whose content is intended to be included within your contract; rather than merge both documents, it is just named and referred to instead.

EXAMPLE 4.12

The contract dated November 15, 2015 and titled United States Visa Support Document by and between Artist and the Young Artist Development Program Sponsor is incorporated by reference into this contract and shall be made part of this Artist Employment Contract.

Clauses Commonly Found in Musicians' Contracts

The clauses discussed in this chapter are those most commonly found in musicians' professional contracts. For each type, you will see at least one example, alternative names for the clause (because sometimes different people refer to the same clause by different names), what *type* of contract it is likely to be found in, what its *purpose* is in that contract, what to be cautious about, and tips for negotiating alternative language, if relevant.

Identifying these clauses and understanding how they operate in the context of the contract is critically important because these clauses, taken as a whole, will expand or contract your rights. Keep in mind that titles are not commonly given within the contract itself, so you'll have to read each clause, identify it, and determine its function in the contract in consideration of all of the other clauses.

It's not easy, but being armed with this knowledge will help you determine whether the contract is right for you, what risks you are assuming or rights you are waiving if you sign it, and whether you are being adequately compensated as a consequence of taking those risks or by waiving those rights.

For an annotated *presenter's engagement (gig) contract*, see Chapter 7. That example is a classical musician's recital contract. See Chapter 8 for an annotated non-classical musician's *artist-management contract* that contains clauses common to that type of business arrangement. Though the example provided is specific to a non-classical artist, expect to see the same clauses in a classical musician's contract minus the non-classical references.

Throughout this chapter you'll see the words *clauses* and *provisions* used. Clauses are the actual paragraphs in a contract that provide for something— either a duty (an obligation such as performing at a venue), a right (such as the right to be paid for performing), or a restriction (such as an Amendment Clause, which says you may not make any changes to the contract unless the other party agrees to those changes in writing).

Provisions is sometimes used interchangeably with *clauses*, but a provision is the idea or concept of something, whereas the clause is the actual embodiment of that idea or concept. So, the restriction against making changes to the contract is an *Amendment Provision* that is contained in the *Amendment Clause*.

AGENCY CLAUSE

EXAMPLE 5.1

Artist engages Manager to provide services as Artist's represen- tative, personal manager and consultant to direct Artist's career as a vocalist in opera, recital, oratorio, symphonic and all areas of music and theatrical industry including, but not limited to . . .

Note

The Agency Clause spells out that you are engaging the manager to act as your agent (in the general sense—not in the talent/booking agent sense). This rather general clause requires the details contained in other clauses, such as the Power of Attorney and Scope of Engagement Clauses, to narrow the authority down to specific acts in specific instances.

You are hiring the manager to act on your behalf and bind you to contracts as your legal representative. Under general rules of Agency Law, the principal (you) and agent (manager) relationship can be terminated by the principal (you) at any time unless the contract says otherwise. These kinds of contracts generally state when the artist may terminate the contractual relationship; see Termination Clause, Example 5.57.

Caution

Look out for Agency Coupled with an Interest language (see Example 5.2).

An Agency Coupled with an Interest provides for an exception to the general rule of Agency Law. An Agency Coupled with an Interest restricts the principal's ability to terminate the agency agreement until certain financial requirements have been met. In other words, it aims to make the agency relationship irrevocable by you.

An example of this concept might be a scenario where the manager has made a financial investment in the artist by way of a loan (the "interest"). If the contractual arrangement requires that the artist work to repay the loan, the artist cannot freely terminate the agency agreement until the loan has been repaid.

States use different legal tests for how they treat these clauses and whether they will allow them to stand when challenged. I've heard it said that they are rare in performers' contracts, but I've now seen them three times in New York artist-management contracts even though there is a very real question of their validity in this context.

EXAMPLE 5.2

Artist agrees that the only adequate consideration for Manager to accept employment hereunder is full compensation; it being understood that Artist is intending to create an agency coupled with an interest which Manager hereby acknowledges and accepts.

Tip

If you see the Agency Coupled with an Interest phrase in a contract that you are asked to sign with an artist manager, know that he is attempting to restrict your ability to terminate the power you would contractually give him to act on your behalf and collect a fee for doing so. Ask why the clause is in the contract and what the manager's concerns are, if any. If you can't get it removed, speak with an attorney, who may be able to negotiate it out on your behalf or minimize its effect by negotiating a Phase-Out Clause for you as a compromise (see Example 5.35).

ADVANCES CLAUSE

Artist will pay Producer $X for Producer's services hereunder as follows: (1) one-half within forty-eight (48) hours of commencement of recording the masters; and (2) the remaining amount within forty-eight (48) hours of delivery of commercially acceptable masters by Producer to Artist. Any advances paid to Producer hereunder shall constitute advances and, as such, be recoupable from any and all royalties due under this Agreement.

Note
This clause reflects the intent of the parties that the producer be paid something up front for his services so that he doesn't have to wait until the recording is released and royalty payments are eventually distributed in order to be paid.

Tip
Don't confuse an advance with a per diem. An advance is part of your fee that is given to you early—in advance of your work. A per diem is extra money for daily living expenses and is in addition to your fee. Be certain that your engagement (gig) contracts get this right, because if what is actually a per diem is called an advance, you will likely have to pay your manager commission on it and per diems usually are not commissionable unless you and your manager have an unusual commission arrangement.

AMENDMENT CLAUSE

This Agreement shall not be changed, amended, altered or modified. Similarly, no additions, deletions or substitutions will be valid unless such changes, amendments, alterations, modifications, additions, deletions or substitutions are made in writing and duly signed by both parties.

Note

Amendment Clauses can more accurately be characterized as restrictions against making unilateral changes to a contract. Where amending is allowed, the clause will state the manner in which an amendment would be permissible, as this one does.

It's common to see many synonyms used in contracts. In addition to the historical reasons discussed in Chapter 4, another reason is to safeguard against a reader-in-bad-faith saying, "I saw that the contract said I couldn't amend it, but I didn't amend it. I just added to it."

Amendment Clauses are generally not negotiable because allowing people to unilaterally change the contract's terms runs contrary to having a contract (with set terms) in the first place.

Tip

Duly signed means that everything was completed correctly according to the contract provisions themselves. So, if the contract requires a witness and a notary, then *duly signed*, in that instance, means that the signing was witnessed and notarized pursuant to the contract's requirements.

ARBITRATION CLAUSE

> **EXAMPLE 5.5**
>
> Any dispute arising out of this Agreement will be resolved by an arbitrator appointed by the American Arbitration Association with recognized expertise in *XYZ*. The arbitrator will resolve the dispute in accordance with the Commercial Arbitration Rules.

Note

Arbitration Clauses are, in essence, Forum Clauses because they also set the location for the hearing of disputes. But with arbitration, it's the location of the arbitration proceeding, not the location of the court proceeding.

Arbitration is one type of alternative dispute resolution (ADR). It's an alternative to litigation. In arbitration, the parties submit their dispute to one or more third parties to review the issues and settle the matter.

Arbitration is a doubled-edged sword. Arbitration costs are lower than litigation costs and arbitrators tend to be more commercially savvy and predictable than juries, but they also tend to favor commercial interests, which, of course, works against the "little guys"—particularly those who might be presenting an emotional argument for themselves.

Arbitrations are conducted according to sets of rules that vary from place to place, as court rules do. For this reason, the Arbitration Clause also operates as a Forum Clause. The set of rules typically selected are those of the American Arbitration Association, but they need not be.

Arbitration also allows substantial freedom for parties to agree on the laws, procedures, and rules that will apply to the dispute without regard to what is standard in that jurisdiction.

Finally, depending on the jurisdiction and other considerations, there is more opportunity for confidentiality with arbitration because, unlike lawsuits, which as legal proceedings are matters of public record, arbitration proceedings are private. Confidentiality is especially important for non-profit organizations that do not want disputes with artists (or donors) made public because they want to maintain goodwill.

It's common for arbitrators to be retired judges. Often, it's a scenario where there are three arbitrators—one chosen by each party to the dispute and the third chosen by the other two arbitrators. One benefit of arbitrating disputes in the context of performers' contracts is the likelihood of having arbitrators knowledgeable of the business practices common to the arts. So, ADR is a means of cost containment and can be an important way of keeping the costs of products and services at competitive levels.

ASSIGNMENT CLAUSE

EXAMPLE 5.6

Manager retains the right to assign his duties hereunder to an entity in which Manager has a controlling interest.

Note

Assignment Clauses address whether, and to the extent which, one or more of the parties to a contract can or cannot delegate her rights or duties to another person (or entity) who is not a party to the contract.

These clauses either restrict assignment or they contractually allow it. Example 5.6 is *unilateral*. It gives only the manager the right to delegate his contractual responsibilities. So, in this example, the manager is contractually allowed to assign his duties (those services laid out in the Scope of Engagement Clause) to a company he owns or in which he has a majority ownership interest. In this version of an Assignment Clause, the artist can object but has no right to stop the assignment.

Caution

I've seen this clause titled several different ways, sometimes cleverly disguised with an innocuous title like "Controlling Entity." Clauses like this one aren't necessarily bad, but you may especially like the way your chosen manager represents you, so you may not want him to delegate to someone else or to pass your management contract off to another entity.

Tip

If you are uncomfortable with giving this right so broadly to your manager, you can:

1. ask for it to be removed completely. In Chapter 7 you will learn that these types of contracts are personal services contracts, so even if the contract is silent on this issue, your consent will be required before the manager can delegate her contractual responsibilities to a third party; or
2. ask that the clause be amended to require your prior written consent so that you can approve of the person (or entity) to whom the manager intends to delegate her duties (see Example 5.7); or
3. ask that the clause be amended to say that if the manager does delegate her responsibilities, she continues to be responsible to you in overseeing that the professional services you are paying for (and which are enumerated in the Scope of Engagement Clause) are competently carried out (see Example 5.8).

EXAMPLE 5.7

Subject to Artist's prior written consent, Manager may assign her duties hereunder to an entity in which Manager has a controlling interest.

EXAMPLE 5.8

This Agreement may only be assigned by Manager to an entity in which Manager has a majority interest; provided however, that Manager shall remain responsible to Artist for the services contracted hereunder and see that each is competently performed.

EXAMPLE 5.9

This Agreement may not be assigned or transferred without the prior written consent of both Artist and Presenter.

Note

Example 5.9 is from a *presenter's engagement (gig) contract*. This clause is *bilateral*. It restricts *either* party from assigning their duties to another unless the other has first agreed to that assignment in writing. So, in this example, the artist is not allowed to unilaterally substitute another musician to perform in his place and, similarly, the presenter is not allowed to unilaterally assign its right to the artist's performance to another venue/presenter.

AUDIT CLAUSE

Manager may audit Artist's books and records pertaining to the payment of all commissions to Manager once per calendar year up to three (3) years after the date each such accounting is rendered to Manager.

Note

Sometimes titled "Accounting," an Audit Provision gives your manager the right to audit your financial records (or, more likely, your new manager's records) once your contractual relationship with her has ended. The manager wants to be sure that the commissions that she is still receiving from you are the full amount due her.

Caution

Don't confuse this provision with the Recordkeeping Clause discussed in Example 5.38. Recordkeeping Provisions generally give rights to artists. Audit Provisions generally give rights to the manager.

Tip

This clause can more accurately be titled a Post-Contract Audit Clause because that's how it operates—once the contractual relationship is over between artist and manager and where artist continues to have to pay manager a commission, the Audit Clause gives the manager the right to audit financial books relating to artist's work in order to confirm that full commissions are being paid to him.

BUNDLED CLAUSE

CHOICE OF LAW

This agreement, construed, interpreted and governed pursuant to the laws of New York State, is a complete and accurate manifestation of the understandings between the parties. It cannot be changed orally and can only be amended, modified or waived in writing, signed by both parties.

Note

I call clauses like this one bundled clauses. They are many clauses in which two or more ideas are being represented in the same clause. Example 5.11 contains four distinct ideas: (1) a New York Choice of Law Clause, (2) a Merger Clause, (3) an Amendment Clause, and (4) a Waiver Clause.

Caution

This is a great example of the importance of reading and understanding every clause in your contracts and provides a specific caution against relying on what the clause titles/headings say because the titles, if any, usually refer only to the first provision contained in the bundle.

CHOICE OF LAW CLAUSE

It is the intention of the parties that the validity, construction, performance, and application of this Agreement shall be governed exclusively by the laws of the City of New York, County of New York, State of New York.

Note

The Choice of Law Clause is also referred to as a Governing Law Clause. Some industries use Choice of Law Clauses more than others. Because contract law is a matter of state law, some states may have laws that are more favorable to that industry than others, so it's a good idea for companies to be aware of state differences and have a favorable state's law apply to the subject matter of their contracts. Understanding what the law provides and how a court might apply the law removes some of the murkiness inherent in a state's business environment and thus becomes a factor in the pricing of a company's goods and services.

In the context of the types of professional contracts that performers sign, the choice of law is frequently New York or California because of the relative familiarity that courts in those states have with the business practices of performers and other creative people.

If your contract has a Choice of Law Clause that seems out of place given where the drafting party is located and where the contract is to be performed, you likely won't know the reasoning for it unless you ask. But it's safe to assume that there is some financial benefit to the other party for that choice.

More important than which state's laws will apply to a potential dispute is the location of where the dispute will be heard (see Forum Clause, Example 5.25).

COMMISSION CLAUSE

EXAMPLE 5.13

Artist agrees to pay Manager X percent (X%) of Artist's "gross income" except with respect to appearances in operas or operatic productions in which event Manager's compensation shall be Y percent (Y%) of artist's "gross income" regardless of when payment is received or to whom payment is made for any and all agreements for Artist's professional services.

Note

The Commission Clause is a very important one, of course, because it lays out the fee structure the manager will collect when you start to work. The permissible commission rates that a licensed talent agent can charge are often determined by state law, but for managers, the rates are dictated by custom.

Caution

As noted above, when it comes to commissions in artist-management agreements, there is so little uniformity with respect to commission amounts that it is impossible to provide a suggested schedule here.

Tip

Ask your colleagues what is standard today, noting the distinctions between genres (classical, jazz, popular, etc.); presentation types (opera, oratorio, musical theater, etc.); and geography (inside or outside the United States).

Regarding the clause itself, look for the following:

1. the percentage fee paid to the manager for various types of engagements;
2. whether your engagement fees are to be paid to the manager (on your behalf) or to you directly. If your fees are to be paid to the manager, the Commission Clause may allow for the manager to take his percentage out before sending the balance to you.

Caution

Some artist-management contracts provide that if the artist is paid her fee directly, she has X days to remit the manager's commission percentage; if this amount is not remitted within X number of days of receipt by the artist, it will be considered a loan by the manager and interest charges may apply.

Caution

The Commission Clause should use a defined term such as *gross income* (as Example 5.13 does), *gross earnings*, or something similar to identify, as specifically as possible, what income or earnings are commissionable.

Some contracts will include salaries, prize money, royalties, and residuals as being subject to the manager's commission. In other words, you would have to pay a percentage of your teaching salary if you are invited to teach for a semester at a conservatory; income from master class work; competition winnings; licensing income, if any, from publishing; or income from your work appearing in a commercial or print advertisement. Is this OK with you?

Tip

If you object to some of these inclusions, you are entitled to negotiate lesser percentages. For longer-term gigs, like a professorship or a Broadway show, you may want to negotiate a Phase-Out Clause that would apply to any long-term arrangements that might come your way (see Example 5.35), but consider the extent to which your manager has bolstered your career to the level that a university or Broadway theater became interested in you in the first place. Minimally, if your manager was instrumental in negotiating a higher salary for, say, your professorship, he or she should be entitled to some compensation, but 10% of your salary over decades may be excessive.

Consider these issues before you sign a contract containing an excessively broad Commission Clause (which is precisely what you will have if you don't require a definition of *gross income* or *gross earnings* that is specifically tailored to your needs and interests).

CONSTRUCTION CLAUSE

EXAMPLE 5.14

Titles or captions of sections contained in this contract have been inserted as a matter of convenience and in no way define, limit, extend, describe or otherwise affect the scope or meaning of this contract or the intent of any provisions hereof.

Note

Sometimes referred to as Headings, Captions or Titles clauses, actual headings or titles over individual contract clauses are rare. When they are provided they can be misleading because, for lack of space, they usually indicate only what the first part of the clause does. Construction Clauses simply state that the headings, captions, or titles (if provided at all) in the contract are there to help readers maneuver around the contract and are not to be construed as having any special meaning.

The reason for clauses like this one is to avoid ambiguity between the naming convention used for the heading and how the clause is intended to operate in the contract. For example, some clauses may bundle together several concepts, but the title given to that clause may be an accurate reflection of only the first concept in the clause.

EXAMPLE 5.15

GOVERNING LAW

This agreement, construed, interpreted and governed pursuant to the laws of New York State, is a complete and accurate manifestation of the understandings between the parties. It cannot be changed orally and can only be amended, modified or waived in writing, signed by both parties.

Caution

Example 5.15 is titled "Governing Law," but it actually accomplishes several things: it contains (1) a New York Choice of Law Clause, (2) a Merger Clause, (3) an Amendment Clause, and (4) a Waiver Clause. This is a great example of the importance of reading and understanding every clause rather than relying on what the clause titles/headings say.

Tip

Never rely solely on the headings or titles given to individual clauses in any kind of contract because they may be inaccurate, incomplete, or misleading.

DEFAULT CLAUSE

EXAMPLE 5.16

In the event of a default hereunder, the aggrieved party will send written notice to the other party outlining the nature of the alleged default and provide two (2) calendar weeks for the other party to cure the alleged default before taking steps to terminate this Agreement.

Note

The Default Clause, if one exists, will outline what you should do if you believe that the other party is not performing his or her duties under the contract. Both parties must follow these formalities. Default provisions often outline *how* one party is required to notify the other when they believe the other is in default and often provide a period of time (called a cure period, which in Example 5.16 is two weeks) for the defaulting party to take steps to cure the default, if they choose to, once they've been notified.

So, these clauses often have two parts: (1) provide details, in writing, about what your issues are with me; and (2) give me a specific time frame to try to change my behavior. Only then can the aggrieved party allege that the other party is in *breach of contract.*

These provisions are important because they encourage the parties to a contract to work out their differences in order to avoid breach and preserve the business relationship; see Chapter 3 for a discussion of breach.

Tip

A contract without a Default Clause isn't necessarily a bad thing. It just means that there are no formal requirements built into the contract for you to follow to get your manager back on track, if that is what's needed. If you do have a grievance with your manager, producer, or presenter, it's best to keep detailed records of your conversations (with dates) outlining what was said and what promises were made. If verbal communication doesn't fix things, follow a more formal approach by notifying the individual in writing about your issues with her and the steps you've taken to address the issues to no avail; see Chapter 9 for guidance.

DISCHARGE (FROM EMPLOYMENT) CLAUSE

EXAMPLE 5.17

Employer has the right to discharge any Artist for cause or for the bona fide violation of any of Employer's personnel policies, so long as those policies are applied uniformly to all the Employer's employees.

Note

Clauses like the one in Example 5.17 are common to Collective Bargaining Agreements like those between musician unions and their signatory companies. The Discharge Clause clarifies for the artist that despite having an employment contract, she can still be fired for good reason such as not being prepared, being consistently late, damaging property, etc.

EXCLUSIVITY CLAUSE

EXAMPLE 5.18

Artist understands and agrees that the Artist is appointing and engaging Manager on an exclusive basis.

Note

Exclusivity Clauses are common in artist-management contracts. The nature of the arrangement is that managers generally have several artists they represent, but artists generally have only one manager (or at least one in a given geographic territory) to represent them.

Caution

Sometimes personal representative contracts indicate a specific territory that the manager/agent's (exclusive) services apply. See Territory Clause, Example 5.59.

Tip

When an overseas territory is indicated in the contract, the reality is that it is common for a local representative be involved. So, your Exclusivity Clause will need to be waived in such instances. If you anticipate performing abroad, ask your manager/agent how the commission structure will work.

But generally, ask why the territory needs to be so broad. Ask what connections the manager has outside the United States and who from her roster has performed in those countries and what those artists' experiences were there, generally, and with respect to engagement fees, commissions, and taxes. Maybe you can contact those artists to inquire directly.

Anecdotal information I've been given is that the two representatives will negotiate a split of the commission you pay, but this may not be common—you may end up paying a larger commission to perform abroad. Determine these details in advance of accepting such work and be sure to speak with a tax professional to determine what your tax liability will be to local (foreign) and U.S. authorities. You need to be convinced that the net amount of the fee you will receive for performing abroad will be worth it in light of the increased expenses.

EXAMPLE 5.19

Composer agrees to grant Commissioning Body the exclusive right of performance of the composition for a period of fifteen (15) months after the premiere performance only if Presenter obtains the requisite funding as indicated in item X, above.

Note

This Exclusivity Clause is taken from a commission contract between a composer and an orchestra. While the orchestra has committed to performing the premiere of the commissioned work, it is apparently uncertain whether it can play subsequent public performances of it. Those later performances are conditioned upon the orchestra's ability to raise funding.

To protect its financial investment in this piece, the orchestra is contractually restricting the composer's ability to allow other organizations to play this work for a period of fifteen months after its premiere. In other words, if the orchestra is able to raise the funding to play the piece again, it wants to be able to sell tickets to those performances in order to offset the cost of the commission.

EXAMPLE 5.20

Artist agrees that, for the duration of Artist's engagement hereunder, Artist will not become involved in any other business ventures that may compete with Presenter's operations or will or may adversely affect Artist's performance under this Agreement.

Note

In Example 5.20, the presenter seems to be interested in restricting the artist's business activities in order to preserve its ticket sales.

An article in the March 2, 2005, *New York Times* is illustrative of the concept of exclusivity. The article, titled "The Exclusive Soprano," tells the story of the opera singer, Deborah Voigt, who was caught up in the competitive classical music market of Minneapolis/St. Paul. Apparently, her Schubert Club–sponsored vocal recital at the Ordway Center in St. Paul had to be canceled just a few days after it was initially advertised because Ms. Voigt had an Exclusivity Clause in her contract with the Minnesota Orchestra (of Minneapolis) seven months later in which she was contracted to sing arias from Puccini's *Tosca*. The orchestra enforced the Exclusivity Clause within its contract with Ms. Voigt despite the difference in program material and time between the two scheduled performances.

EXCULPATORY CLAUSE

EXAMPLE 5.21

Presenter shall have no liability and Artist shall hold Presenter harmless for any and all injuries including, but not limited to physical, emotional, psychological or financial injuries sustained by Artist as a result of Presenter's actual or alleged negligent acts or the actual or alleged negligent acts of Presenter's agents, representatives, employees and subcontractors which occurred during the preparation for or performance(s) of the production to which this Agreement applies.

Note

An Exculpatory Clause is similar to an Indemnification Clause, except an Exculpatory Provision excuses some behavior by the other party.

Example 5.21 is from a *presenter's engagement contract* in which the artist is agreeing, in advance, not to sue the presenter or the presenter's affiliates for their negligence. For example, if presenter was negligent in providing a well-lit backstage area and the artist tripped and was injured, the artist has already agreed to not bring a lawsuit against the presenter for their negligence. It's difficult to say whether, in this example, the exculpation would actually be enforceable.

Caution

This clause could just be there as a deterrent to a lawsuit, generally, or it may, in practice, serve to limit any *damages* awarded to the injured artist if she did sue the presenter despite this clause in her contract.

EXTENSION CLAUSE

EXAMPLE 5.22

Artist understands and agrees that Manager shall have the sole and exclusive right to extend this Agreement for a period of one (1) year upon the natural termination of this Agreement.

Note

An Extension Clause governs the opportunity to extend the contract under certain situations, such as one conditioned upon the artist reaching some professional milestone—winning a prestigious award or being booked into a Broadway show, for example.

Caution

Example 5.22 is a *unilateral* Extension Clause. Recall from Chapter 4 that unilateral clauses are those that are one-sided. In other words, they benefit one party over another. This example gives the manager the sole right to extend the contract. Contrast that version with the *bilateral* version, where either can elect to extend the contract.

Either party may extend this Agreement for a period of one (1) year upon the natural termination of this Agreement.

Tip

Unilateral clauses are not always bad; sometimes they make sense. When you come across one, ask yourself whether a bilateral version of the same clause makes sense or not. If making the unilateral language bilateral makes sense to you and you prefer it, ask that the clause be amended to be fully bilateral like the version in Example 5.23.

Caution

Before taking a knee-jerk approach to asking that a clause like this one be made bilateral, consider the reality of this situation: the only thing that changes by making the Extension Clause bilateral is that you, as the artist, get the right to decide if you want the contract extended and can do so without the manager's interest in an extension.

Do you really want to force the manager to an extension if he is not really interested in representing you? I wouldn't want that.

Tip

Another solution would be to just remove the clause entirely. This way, after this contract runs its course, if you and your manager *both* want the business relationship to continue, you can draw up another contract. This solution will also give you the opportunity to negotiate changes to your new contract for anything that you didn't like in the first one.

FORCE MAJEURE CLAUSE

Neither party shall be liable to the other for damages arising out of the non-performance of this Agreement resulting from Acts of God including lightning, hail, fire, volcanic action, earthquake, labor strike or civil insurrection which shall be deemed beyond the control of both parties to this Agreement.

Note

Also referred to as the "Acts of God" or the "Acts of Nature" Clause, the Force Majeure Clause excuses performance by both parties under the contract due to the impossibility of performance because of one or more of the stated occurrences. Originally, these were limited to true natural events like hurricanes or mudslides, but in modern times, the clause continues to expand to include any number of things, including terrorist acts and labor strikes.

Tip

Read the story in the preface about the genesis of this book (and additional references to it in Chapter 3) for a real-life example of how one arts organization attempted (unsuccessfully) to use a Force Majeure Clause to avoid its contractual obligation to pay a stage director his fee.

When reviewing your contract, be sure that there isn't content within this clause that could turn your contract into an illusory promise. An illusory promise is a fake promise that sounds like a real promise, but is not binding and, therefore, cannot serve as the basis for a valid, enforceable contract. Recall from Chapter 2 that a valid contract must contain promises made by each party to the other. If one party to the contract isn't truly promising to do anything, then no valid contract exists.

One example could be something in this clause that states that the organization "may" mount a production or that a program is "under consideration." These are not binding promises.

Distinguish non-binding promises from conditions that must be satisfied before a promise can be binding. For example, an organization may condition hiring you on first obtaining a grant or other funding. Conditions that must be met before a binding promise is triggered are valid. For example, "If you graduate from your program with a minimum GPA of 3.5, I will hire you to work for me." The binding promise of hiring you doesn't spring to life until the GPA condition is met.

FORUM CLAUSE

EXAMPLE 5.25

In the event of a dispute arising hereunder, the venue for resolution shall be the First Department of the Supreme Court of New York, New York County.

Note

A venue-setting provision, also known as a Forum Clause, is akin to a Choice of Law Clause. It lays out, in advance of a dispute, the specific court where any contract disputes will be heard. It is common for contracts involving actors, musicians, and other creative people in the northeastern United States to have a New York County Forum Clause because these courts have experience hearing these types of cases and are familiar with the business practices, unions, and other issues involving such persons and their business arrangements.

Forum Clauses are useful to the contract drafter as a cost-containment measure because if a business is headquartered in City X, it will be cheaper to bring legal actions to enforce its contractual rights in a forum in City X, rather than having to travel to another part of the country to do the same thing.

Ideally, the forum for dispute resolution is local to you so that if issues do arise, it won't be impractically expensive for you to travel there should you need to. If the forum is not local, try to negotiate a forum that is more economically feasible for you, but recognize for the reasons discussed above that choosing a more convenient forum may not be possible. If you are stuck with a Forum Clause that is in a jurisdiction to which is financially impractical for you to travel to enforce your rights under the contract, determine for yourself whether the value of the contract to you is worth the risk of not being able to enforce your rights should the need arise.

GROSS INCOME DEFINITION

EXAMPLE 5.26

Gross income includes, but is not limited to earnings, advances, teaching opportunities, salaries, cash prizes, stocks, bonds, cash, sales, royalties, leases, bonuses and all other emoluments regardless of form of payment.

Note

This definition is often embedded within the Commission Clause. If a definition is provided (and it should be), it tells you what the manager considers to be commissionable income. Knowing what work is subject to commission is too important to leave to interpretation. It should be defined. Recall from Chapter 4 that whenever a term is being defined in a contract, its meaning is being narrowed.

It's uncommon to see living expense per diems included in a definition of *gross income* (subject to manager's commission percentage). But I have seen a clause that states that to the extent that the manager negotiated a higher per diem for an artist than what was originally offered, then that increased amount would be commissionable even if the original per diem amount is not. In contrast, an advance, if truly an advance against your fee for whatever purpose, should be commissionable.

Caution

Some of these clauses are carelessly drafted and include both *advances* and *per diems*. Advances are that—advance payment of a portion of your engagement fee. Per diems, by contrast, are help with living expenses—often a daily or weekly amount that the artist can use as he/she wishes. If the world you perform in is one where per diems are provided by presenters, make sure that per diems are not included within the definition of *gross income* in your artist-management contract because if they are, you will pay commission on those amounts. Advances are always commissionable because they are part of your engagement fee.

Tip

Consider what you want to be subject to commission and what you would like to be specifically excluded. Negotiate with the manager on this point. At minimum, you can agree upon reduced percentages in some instances (maybe on gigs where you accept a lower fee than usual—such as for a charity event) or a Phase-Out Clause in other, potentially longer-term commissions (such as a university teaching position or a Broadway show). See Example 5.35 for a Phase-Out Clause.

Caution

If you are a composer/songwriter: While it's not uncommon for royalties to be built into the definition of *gross income* and, therefore, be commissionable, watch out for *transfer of rights* language in your contracts. If you are asked to sign over your ownership interest in something you've created, such as a copyright, don't do it unless you are intending to forever give up your ownership of it. If your actual intention is to let someone use something you've created, you most likely are intending to give that person or organization a *grant of rights* (a license), not an outright transfer of your ownership interest in it. The license you give can be exclusive to that person or organization or not. Also, you can limit the license by duration (e.g., a year) or by geography (e.g., the United States).

In Example 5.26, the word *leases* is included within the definition of *gross income*. I believe that the drafter of this clause intends for the term *leases* to encompass music licensing grants. For example, if a portion of a piece of music you wrote was licensed as background music for a television show or film, that licensing income would be commissionable under this definition.

Tip

The term *leases* in Example 5.26 should be defined because it clearly has more than one meaning.

INDEMNIFICATION CLAUSE

Artist shall defend, indemnify and hold Presenter, its officers, employees and agents harmless from and against any and all liability, loss, expense (including reasonable attorney's fees) or claims for injury or damages arising out of the performance of this Agreement but only in proportion to and to the extent such liability, loss, expense, attorney's fees or claims for injury or damages are caused by or result from the negligent or intentional acts or omissions of Artist, its officers, agents or employees.

Presenter shall defend, indemnify and hold Artist, its officers, employees and agents harmless from and against any and all liability, loss, expense (including reasonable attorney's fees) or claims for injury or damages arising out of the performance of this Agreement but only in proportion to and to the extent such liability, loss, expense, attorney's fees or claims for injury or damages are caused by or result from the negligent or intentional acts or omissions of Presenter, its officers, agents or employees.

Note

Also known as Hold Harmless Provisions, Indemnification Clauses say that you agree to provide a legal defense for (hire an attorney to represent) and to indemnify (pay any monetary judgment awarded) if a third party successfully sues both you and the other person/entity relating to the promises made to one another under the contract.

In the case of a presenter's contract, the artist is agreeing to provide a legal defense and pay for any judgment rendered against the presenter as the result of the artist's appearance at the presenter's venue.

For example, you have contracted to perform a recital and have provided program notes about the music to the presenter to distribute to the audience. Someone in attendance claims that your program notes are plagiarized and sues you and the presenter for copyright infringement. Via the Indemnification Clause in your contract, you have agreed to hire an attorney to respond to this lawsuit and represent both yourself and the presenter. If the suit is successful against both of you, you are also responsible for paying the presenter's share of any judgment awarded.

It is important to understand what you are agreeing to in this kind of provision. The clause very likely opens the parties up to liability that is more than the value of the contract. You may not be able to have it removed, but if the clause unilaterally benefits the other party, you should at least ask for it to be made equal (bilateral) to benefit you in the same exact way.

Example 5.27 is bilateral. You'll notice the mirrored effect of the language, which shows that both the presenter and the artist have the very same obligations—to defend and indemnify each other. See Chapter 4 for a discussion of unilateral and bilateral clauses and other forms of limiting language.

KEY MAN CLAUSE

EXAMPLE 5.28

It is understood and agreed that in the event Manager ceases to be employed by X; ceases to be primarily responsible for providing services on Artist's behalf; or is no longer directly involved in the day-to-day activities in support of Artist's career as enumerated in the Scope of Engagement section of this Agreement, Artist shall have the have the right to terminate this Agreement upon thirty (30) days' written notice.

Note

Its politically incorrect name notwithstanding, this provision recognizes the notion that some artists are particularly fond of a specific individual within their management agency—a person with whom the artist has developed a personal relationship and built a level of trust. The Key Man Clause allows for the artist to terminate the agreement and change agencies if her specific manager dies, quits the business, or moves to a new agency. I like this clause because it gives the artist the option of leaving an agency if she is unhappy for reasons related to her manager's departure.

Tip
Artists who have this clause written into their artist-management contracts should keep in mind that even though the option of following the manager to another agency may be possible, other factors can interfere. If the manager has an employment contract with the original organization, he may have a non-compete clause written into that contract that precludes him from taking artists with him for a specified time period or in a specified geographic region.

MERGER CLAUSE

EXAMPLE 5.29

This Agreement constitutes the entire understanding between the parties and shall supersede all prior agreements, arrangements, negotiations, proposals and understandings, if any, relating to the obligations and matters set out herein, whether oral or written.

Note
Sometimes called an Integration Clause and sometimes titled "Entire Agreement" (if a title is used at all), the Merger Clause is very important. It states that the contract, as written, is the full and complete embodiment of both parties' understanding of the arrangement and, as such, operates to exclude from evidence any contradictory side deals made during negotiations—whether written or oral.

In other words, if during negotiations you were told something other than what is spelled out in the contract, then even if you had a signed note to that effect that predates the contract signing, the Merger Clause would preclude the introduction of that evidentiary note.

For example, you have contracted to work at a summer arts festival to teach a studio of ten students and to participate, as a faculty member, in three public performances. You have a signed contract outlining these responsibilities. During contract negotiations you exchanged e-mails with a festival administrator who said that if the final studio numbers rose above 12 students, you would receive an additional fee for your time. If your contract has a Merger Clause, you would be prevented from introducing those e-mails as evidence that you are entitled to the additional fee for the additional teaching responsibilities. The Merger Clause prevents the introduction of any contradictory evidence, oral or written, that predates the contract signing date.

However, if you encounter such a side deal *after* the contract is signed, ask that the original contract be amended, or ask for a separate contract that contains the details relating to that side deal that *incorporates by reference* the original contract. See chapter 4 for a discussion and example of incorporation by reference.

NON-EXCLUSIVITY CLAUSE

EXAMPLE 5.30

Artist understands and agrees that Manager is non-exclusive to artist and, as such, will perform the same or similar professional services for others during the term of this Agreement.

Note

Expect to see a clause that says something to the effect that the Manager will perform the same services for others as he does for you. These clauses are often followed by another clause that states that artist agrees to be exclusive to the manager. The nature of the arrangement is that managers generally have several artists they represent, but artists generally have only one manager (or at least one in a given geographic territory) to represent them; see Exclusivity Clause, Example 5.18.

Caution

Read such clauses carefully because sometimes they are worded very broadly and can allow managers to work in completely different fields—something that may not interest you. Know whether your manager represents artists only on a part-time basis and really makes the bulk of his livelihood doing something else. You may not want to be represented by someone who is inexperienced or whose company's financial viability comes from monthly retainer income paid by you and the other artists on the roster.

EXAMPLE 5.31

Artist understands and agrees that Manager is engaged as a professional in various other business enterprises that in no way shall limit Manager's ability to perform the duties outlined hereunder.

Note

In Example 5.31, the manager is telling you that he/she has (or may have) other business interests. Do you want a manager who could potentially have any conflict of interest between guiding your career and looking out for his own interests in the same creative space? For example, if you are a stage director specializing in operettas, you would want to know if your manager's other enterprises (and income source) is directing regional Gilbert and Sullivan productions.

Tip

Ask for an explanation of what "other business enterprises" the manager is involved in.

EXAMPLE 5.32

Artist engages Producer on a non-exclusive basis to produce and remix individual master recordings of Artist's compositions and performances contained on Artist's album, X, currently under production.

Note

Example 5.32 is taken from an artist-producer agreement. It provides that
while the producer is engaged by the artist, the producer is not exclusive to the
artist. So he can work in the same capacity for other artists during the same
time period as well.

Tip

If you, as the artist employing the producer, are concerned about the producer splitting his time between your project and others' projects, you can
hire the producer on an exclusive basis or, as a compromise, ask for language
to be added to either the Engagement Clause or the Non-exclusivity Clause
that states that the producer's services shall be provided on a non-exclusive,
"first priority" basis to the artist until the producer's material obligations
under the agreement (in other words, his most important responsibilities)
have been met.

PAY OR PLAY CLAUSE

EXAMPLE 5.33

Compensation shall be "PAY OR PLAY" and be paid in United
States currency (a) prior to the commencement of each single
performance or (b) before 6 p.m. on the last day of each performance week.

Note

Pay or Play means that if the job for which the artist is contracted is canceled
or the production is never mounted, the artist will still be entitled to her
full fee. In the context of how musical theater, opera, oratorio, and similar
engagements are contracted, the Pay or Play Clause merely restates what the
law already provides: if you set aside the time in your professional calendar
to perform, you should be paid regardless of whether the production takes
place or not.

But where these clauses tend to be really meaningful is for film actors' contracts, which take a long time to come together and for which there are often many important contingencies that could derail a very expensive project. In that context, it is less clear whether Pay or Play is part of the larger contract or a stand-alone idea that is binding regardless of whether a contract is ever finalized.

PARTNERSHIP CLAUSE

EXAMPLE 5.34

Artist understands and agrees that nothing contained in this Agreement shall be construed to create a partnership hereunder.

Note

Sometimes you'll see a clause clarifying that the arrangement that is subject of the agreement is not a partnership. The reasons for such a clause are twofold:

1. partnerships create both profit sharing (and legal liabilities) that are outside the scope of the usual artist-manager arrangement. Being that the commission schedule is usually based on percentages of artists' gross income, this language clarifies that just because there is a profit-sharing arrangement, it does not rise to the level of being a partnership; and
2. partnerships create a heightened legal duty owed by the partners to each other and to the business enterprise. A partnership, in the context of an artist-manager agreement, would likely create a conflict of interest, being that managers usually represent several artists simultaneously, so it would be impermissible to give an opportunity to one artist above another—there would be too many conflicts in such an arrangement.

Tip

Don't be concerned if your contract doesn't contain language stating that no partnership is intended to be formed. Such language would generally protect managers against unfounded assertions by artists more than be protective of artists.

PHASE-OUT CLAUSE

EXAMPLE 5.35

Manager's Commission shall be paid in full for a period of two (2) years following the expiration of this Agreement and any extensions thereof; following such two-year period, Manager's Commission shall be payable at a twenty-five (25%) percent reduced rate for one (1) year, then payable at a fifty (50%) percent reduced rate for one (1) year, then payable at a seventy-five (75%) percent reduced rate for one (1) year, after which no further Commission payments shall be due.

Note

Sometimes referred to as a Post-Term Commission Clause, this is an example of a Phase-Out Clause. Its name comes from how it operates: the commission due to the manager is *phased out* over time from the full amount to zero.

Don't expect to see a Phase-Out Clause in a short–term contract—they don't make sense there. But they can be useful in longer-term arrangements where artist's earnings will be flowing in long after the artist-management relationship has ended.

In Example 5.35, the artist pays full commission for the first two years of the artist-management contract. Then, if the relationship is discontinued for whatever reason, the commission amount due to the manager in year three is reduced by 25% following termination. The original commission percentage is reduced by 50% in year four and by 75% for all of year five.

Hypothetical Case

Using Example 5.35: Your contract requires that you pay your manager 20% of your gross income. For two years you earn $100,000 and pay your manager

$20,000 each year as the money is earned. Then you decide not to renew your contract with the manager.

Because you are working under contracts that your manager procured and/or negotiated for you during his tenure as your manager, you have to continue to pay his commission whether you have a new manager or not (your new manager is not entitled to charge you commission on those earnings). The Phase-Out Clause walks the commission percentage owed to your former manager down over time—in this case, over three years. These clauses are particularly useful in situations where the full value of a deal can't readily be known at its inception.

So, if your gross income remains the same in years three, four and five, you will pay the following commission amounts:

Year three (@ 25% reduction):	$15,000 due ($20,000 × .75)
Year four (@ 50% reduction):	$10,000 due ($20,000 × .50)
Year five (@ 75% reduction):	$5,000 due ($20,000 × .25)

Tip
Originally developed for recording contracts, where the profits come rolling in long after the handshakes, Phase-Out Clauses can also be useful for artists who sign potentially long-term engagements with presenters like those for Broadway shows.

While these percentages may be subject to custom based on geography and musical genre, they are not set in stone. Negotiate them with your manager before signing the contract, keeping in mind that your manager is entitled to take a commission off all your gross earnings for work procured during her tenure as your manager—not just during the actual term that she is your manager.

POWER OF ATTORNEY CLAUSE

EXAMPLE 5.36

Artist hereby authorizes and appoints Manager as Artist's attorney-in-fact to carry out and execute any and all powers necessary for the fulfillment of this Agreement.

Note

You could be asked to sign to a separate document giving your manager a non-durable[1] power of attorney, or the power may be embedded within the artist-management contract itself. State laws determine the requirements for giving another person your power of attorney.

A power of attorney is an instrument whereby one person (the "principal") gives authority to another (the "attorney-in-fact") to act on the principal's behalf. These documents can be drafted to give very broad or very limited powers. The most common powers given in this context are to: (1) bind the artist to performance contracts, (2) sign checks made out to the artist, (3) make decisions on the artist's behalf with respect to commercial use of the artist's image, and (4) pursue actions to protect the artist's rights, generally.

Caution

Example 5.36 is vaguely broad. It is a better idea to complete a separate, formal power of attorney. States often have statutory rules for how these should be completed. Sometimes they require witnesses and a notary public.

Tip

If you decide to give some rights to your manager via a power of attorney, ask for a separate, formal document and make it very specific according to your comfort level: to sign your name to engagement contracts (and you can limit this by duration or geography, etc.); to cash checks made out to you for work you've done (you can ask for a dollar cap to be put on this); and to handle anything else that you feel will make your professional life easier. But keep in mind that your manager does need to be paid in a timely manner for the work he undertakes on your behalf, so please be reasonable with the limitations you negotiate as respects the power of attorney.

Caution

There are different types of powers of attorney. Some are *revocable* by the person giving the right and some are *irrevocable*. Irrevocable powers of attorney cease only when the grantor dies. I cannot image any scenario where an artist should give (or be asked to give) an irrevocable power of attorney.

For example, if you give your manager an irrevocable power of attorney to cash checks relating to your professional work pursuant to a contract, that power remains with the manager for your entire lifetime, which, of course, can exceed the life of your contract with that manager. It's overkill; don't do it.

PUBLICITY CLAUSE

EXAMPLE 5.37

Actor hereby acknowledges and agrees that Producer shall have the perpetual right to utilize Actor's photograph in publicity and advertising for the Play after the termination of the contract with no additional compensation payable to Actor.

Note

This clause is a release given by the actor to producers to allow the use of the actor's photograph forever (sometimes the words *in perpetuity* are used) and for free.

Tip

Be sure you are willing to forever give up your right of publicity if you sign a contract with one of these clauses in it. The more well-known you become and the more powerful your brand, the more likely people and entities will want to use the rights you gave them early in your career to promote their current business and their own brand from their past affiliation with you.

RECORDKEEPING CLAUSE

EXAMPLE 5.38

Manager agrees to keep timely records of all transactions involving Artist and make such records available to Artist for review or, at Artist's request, send Artist a monthly statement of all transactions relevant to Artist. Manager will retain receipts for all fees and other consideration received by Manager on Artist's behalf. All receipts will contain the date, amount and purpose of the fee and the signature of the person receiving payment of same.

Note

There should be a clause that speaks to recordkeeping that either gives you regular statements or, at minimum, makes all business records relating to you available within a reasonable period of time from your request to view them. Sometimes titled "Audit," this is an important clause because it gives you the periodic right to review the business records that pertain to you.

Caution

Don't confuse this provision with an actual Audit Clause (see Example 5.10), which gives your manager the right to audit your financial records (or, more likely, your new manager's records) once his contractual relationship with you has ended. The manager wants to be sure that the commissions that he is still receiving from you are actually his full payment.

Tip

Regardless of the title given for it, if any, you have to read the clause to figure out what's going on.

In a Recordkeeping Provision, you are given the right to review the manager's business records, but only as they relate to your work. You can negotiate this access to be as frequent as you want, within reason. If the contract gives quarterly access, ask for it to be changed to monthly even if you don't plan to review your records that often. It could be useful to you in the future, and when it comes to artists' legal rights, broader is better.

REMEDIES CLAUSE

EXAMPLE 5.39

All rights and remedies of the parties hereunder are cumulative and not in limitation or restriction of any other right or remedy in law or equity.

Note

Recall from Chapter 3 that a Remedies Clause says that if you become aggrieved with the other party's performance (or non-performance) under the contract, you are agreeing, in advance of a dispute, to what legal options for recourse are available to you. Some Remedies Clauses merely state what the law requires (i.e., that all remedies are available) while others limit the available remedies.

Example 5.39 states that all remedy options are available in the event of a breach of contract despite the reality that specific performance, as one example of an equitable remedy, is *not* available to the presenter because of the public policy considerations discussed in Chapter 2.

EXAMPLE 5.40

If Presenter incurs any claims, damages, other liabilities or costs and expenses relating to the non-appearance of Artist for reasons other than those enumerated above, Artist's liability shall not exceed ten percent (10%) of Artist's fee hereunder (excluding Artist's expenses payable by Presenter hereunder).

Example 5.40 is a Remedies Clause with a 100% cap on liability for the Artist.

EXAMPLE 5.41

[Union] agrees that all Artists have the obligation to fulfill his/her employment contract. [Union] acknowledges that employer has the right to pursue all causes of action other than specific performance available to the employer in instances in which an artist willfully chooses to default on the employment contract.

Note

Example 5.41 is another version of Examples 5.39 and 5.40. It simply states what the law already provides: the equitable remedy of specific performance is not available under a performer's contract because it is a personal services contract. In other words, you cannot be forced to perform, but you can be sued for monetary damages for breaching your contract to perform, and the presenter can obtain an injunction that would legally prevent you from performing elsewhere during that original contracted period.

Note

The phrase *causes of action* within the context of Example 5.41 is another way of saying *remedies*. There are many different types of causes of action. Breach of contract is one; negligence is another. Technically, a cause of action is the *manner* in which a remedy is pursued. Contrary to what many people believe, there must be a legally recognized cause of action in order to bring a lawsuit against someone. In other words, you can't sue someone unless your grievance with them falls into a category that the law already recognizes.

RENEWAL CLAUSE

EXAMPLE 5.42

It is understood and agreed that if any renewal or extension of any agreement procured by or negotiated on Artist's behalf by Manager arises within ninety (90) days after the termination of this Agreement, the term of this Agreement shall be automatically extended to terminate at such time as the renewal or extension terminates.

Note

This clause can more accurately be characterized as an Automatic Renewal Clause. It spells out any conditions that could give rise to an automatic renewal of the contract.

Example 5.42 conditions an automatic renewal of the artist-management contract on an extension or renewal of a presenter's contract that takes place within ninety days of the artist-management contract's expiration. The hypothetical situation below illustrates how renewal clauses operate.

Hypothetical Case

Your manager negotiated a contract for you to perform in a Broadway show that lasted for several months, but the show closed during the term of your artist-management contract. Your artist-management contract expired and you chose not to renew it. You and your manager are financially caught up and amicably go your separate ways.

Two months later the producers of that Broadway show decide to revive it and offer you another contract, which you happily accept. Your artist-management contract was also just revived.

The Renewal Clause (Example 5.42) from your artist-management contract requires that you pay commission to your manager for this gig despite: (1) your original contract with him expired and was not renewed; and (2) this second Broadway contract was provided to you after your artist-management contract expired.

Why? Because the second contract was presented to you within ninety days of the expiration of your artist-management contract. So now, your artist-management contract is back in force and, according to this Renewal Clause, is in effect until the show contract ultimately terminates.

Tip

Read carefully and understand these clauses. If you think they are too restrictive, ask for the time periods to be reduced or ask for a phase-out of commissions that arise from such clauses; see Phase-Out Clause, Example 5.35.

REPRESENTATIONS AND WARRANTY CLAUSE

EXAMPLE 5.43

Artist hereby represents, warrants and agrees that:

(1) artist is not under any material disability, restriction or prohibition, whether contractual or otherwise, with respect to their respective rights to execute this Agreement, grant the rights granted hereunder, and perform each and every material term and provision hereof; and

(2) neither the Masters produced hereunder nor any of the content thereof to the extent furnished by Artist and Producer, respectively, nor the manufacture, sale of or other distribution of Records or sound made from, or derived from such Masters, nor any other exploitation or use thereof, to the extent of Artist's and Producer's respective contributions thereto, and no materials, ideas or other properties furnished by Artist, respectively, and embodied or contained in or used in connection with the Masters shall violate any law or infringe upon any common law or statutory rights of any party, including, without limitation, contractual rights, copyrights and rights of privacy.

Note

Representation and Warranty Clauses are sometimes required by one party to a contract to protect themselves from the other. Example 5.43 is from a producer's agreement in which the producer is requiring the artist to affirmatively state and stand by those statements with respect to several things: (1) that the artist has the requisite mental competence to enter into this agreement; (2) that the artist is not contractually bound to another producer who could allege that this producer is attempting to interfere with the earlier producer's agreement with the same artist; (3) that the artist owns all of the content, such that no viable claims of infringement could come from a third party; (4) that if some of the content contained on the masters is borrowed from another, proper licenses were procured; and (5) that nothing contained in the masters would likely violate any person's right of privacy (such as content inappropriately used from someone's private writings).

EXAMPLE 5.44

Artist warrants and represents that Artist is under no legal disability and has the right to enter into this Agreement and perform its terms. Further, no act or omission by Artist will violate the rights of any person, firm or corporation or will subject Manager to any liability or claims.

Note

Example 5.44 is taken from an artist-management contract. The manager asks for similar guarantees to protect herself from possible claims that the manager coerced the artist to leave another manager and sign with her. This type of unprofessional activity is legally actionable. The legal claim for this is *tortious interference with contract*. The manager is attempting to protect herself from a potential lawsuit alleging that she poached the artist from another manager's roster.

RIGHT OF FIRST REFUSAL CLAUSE

EXAMPLE 5.45

Commissioning Body shall have the right of first refusal of any form of recording of the work for a period of fifteen (15) months after the premiere performance.

Note

Example 5.45 is from a composer's commission contract in which an orchestra commissioned a piece of music from a classical composer. The orchestra (the "commissioning body") has contracted for the right to be the first to record the work, so if any other entity approaches the composer about recording this piece within fifteen months of its premiere, he must go to this orchestra's leadership and give them the first option to make the recording. The orchestra doesn't have to record it; it just has the right to be given the first opportunity to do so.

SAVINGS CLAUSE

EXAMPLE 5.46

In the event that this Agreement or any part of it is unlawful or invalid in any state or country, other than New York, the territory of this Agreement shall automatically be deemed to exclude such state or country and this Agreement shall not otherwise be affected thereby.

Note

Some people use the terms *Savings Clause* and *Severability Clause* interchangeably. I think they are distinct because, to me, a Savings Clause will "save" the individual clause (or the entire contract) from failing by allowing it to be "deemed modified" to conform to the requirements of the law if that becomes necessary.

To my mind, a Severability Clause, by contrast, is a version of a Savings Clause. Rather than deem some language to change to conform to the law, a Severability Clause says that any language that is determined to not be in harmony with the law shall be removed (severed) from the contract and the balance of the language will remain in full force and effect.

EXAMPLE 5.47

To the extent that any provision of this Agreement is determined to be in conflict with any material law, the latter shall prevail.

Note

Example 5.47 is another example of a Savings Clause where a drafter is attempting to save a contract (or a provision in it) from failing. In this example, the drafter is trying to provide for the contract language to be modified if it conflicts with the law in any material (significant) way.

SCOPE OF ENGAGEMENT CLAUSE (LICENSED AGENT VERSION)

EXAMPLE 5.48

Agent's duties shall be to use reasonable efforts to procure and negotiate employment for Artist as *X* in the fields of *WYZ*. Agent may also periodically provide counsel and guidance on Artist's career development as Agent, in Agent's sole discretion, deems necessary.

Note

The Scope of Engagement Clause spells out the details of the work an agent will perform for you. You may see wildly different versions of this clause.

Example 5.48 is typical of a licensed agent's contract. It doesn't have much content because agents, as discussed above, are licensed like employment agencies (where they are regulated at all). Talent/booking agents' primary objective is to procure employment for the artists on their roster. Their secondary objective is to counsel artists and guide their careers. For this reason, the Scope of Engagement Clause for licensed talent/booking agents will be fairly succinct, as this one is, and the actual content of those contracts may be governed by state law. For contrast, see the same clause for an artist manager in Example 5.49.

SCOPE OF ENGAGEMENT CLAUSE (ARTIST MANAGER VERSION, PART A)

EXAMPLE 5.49

Artist engages Manager to render services on Artist's behalf as Artist's personal representative to guide and counsel Artist; as well as develop Artist's career in the fields of operatic, theatrical, concert, oratorio, recital, in all branches of entertainment industry including, but not limited to stage work, symphonic, television, radio, Internet and all other venues.

Manager will also handle all activities in support of Artist's appearances in any of the foregoing including preparing and distributing Artist's promotional materials to the venue in advance of Artist's appearance.

Note

Example 5.49 is a Scope of Engagement Clause from an artist manager's contract for a classical singer. This clause is very important because it is necessary to narrow the broad powers given by the artist to the manager in the Agency Clause (see Example 5.1). This long list of activities in the Scope of Engagement Clause is intended to keep the manager out of trouble with the licensing authorities in states that license agents. The idea is to list all the professional services that are being rendered by the manager to the artist as compensation for a percentage of the artist's income (in other words, "Look at all of the things I do that have nothing to do with procuring employment").

This laundry list will usually be followed somewhere in the contract with a companion clause that expressly states that the manager is not responsible for procuring employment for the artist; see Example 5.53, Scope of Engagement, Part B.

Caution

Watch out for overly broad or vague language in these clauses. You want a manager who will earn that percentage of your income and who will commit to performing specifics tasks in support of your career goals.

Tip

It's important to know the exact services your manager will provide you in exchange for a percentage of your gross income.

My recommendation is to make a list of daily, regularly occurring things you need help with in support of your engagements and, ultimately, in furtherance of your career objectives. Next, compare that list with what the manager actually said she will do for you. For example:

I need help with the following:
- Getting auditions for larger venues to work with more established colleagues
- Meeting key decision-makers
- Getting higher-profile publicity and possibly hiring a publicity manager
- Completing administrative tasks (preparing and mailing press kits, etc.)
- Negotiating contract terms and fees
- Possibly endorsing a high-end product
- Crossing over musical genres to exploit my crossover abilities

Does your list match up with what the manager told you? Is anything missing? Are your expectations accurate and appropriate? Make note of what may be missing from the Scope Clause from the contract you were given to sign.

Next, look at the recitals section of that contract for a high-level view of your manager's contractual responsibilities; see Chapter 4 for a discussion of contract recitals. Example 5.50 is a recital from an artist-management contract.

EXAMPLE 5.50

WHEREAS, Manager desires to assist and help Artist develop Artist's career by handling the day-to-day business of the Artist to allow the Artist to create, write, record, tour and otherwise fully and completely develop Artist's unique talent in the entertainment industry.

Tip

Next, look at the Scope of Engagement Clause. The scope clause should provide details in support of the content found in the recitals.

EXAMPLE 5.51

Manager will:

a. represent Artist, act as negotiator, fix the terms governing matters of disposition, use, employment or exploitation of Artist's talents and the products thereof;

b. supervise Artist's professional employment, consult with employers and prospective employers;

c. exploit Artist's personality in all media; and

d. be available at reasonable times and places to confer with Artist in connection with all matters concerning Artist's professional career, business interests, employment, and publicity.

Note

There's nothing wrong with the recital in Example 5.50 or the Scope of Engagement text in Example 5.51, but it's just a little too high-level for my comfort level. This language suggests to me that this manager doesn't really want to commit to anything specifically.

I would request that it be revised to provide exactly what services you need help with, making sure that the list encompasses everything that the manager told you would be provided to you; see Example 5.52 for a more detailed list.

EXAMPLE 5.52

Manager agrees to provide:

(a) Professional Management activities to:

(1) supervise Artist's professional employment, and on Artist's behalf, to consult with employers and prospective employers so as to assure the proper use of and continued demand for Artist's services;

(2) be available at reasonable times and places to confer with Artist in connection with all matters concerning Artist's professional career, business interests, employment, and publicity;

(3) with Artist's prior approval: engage, discharge and/or direct such theatrical agents, booking agencies and employment agencies, as well as other firms, persons or corporations that may be retained for the purpose of securing contracts, engagements or employment for Artist;

(4) advise, counsel and guide Artist in the strategic management of Artist's career in the Entertainment Industry;

(5) assist Artist in meeting and forming relationships with key decision-makers in the Entertainment Industry relevant to Artist's talent and long-range career plans;

(6) negotiate all contract terms, fees (including per diems where possible) on Artist's behalf and to fix the terms governing matters of disposition, use, employment or exploitation of Artist's talents and the products thereof;

(7) represent Artist in all dealings with any union; and

EXAMPLE 5.52

(8) accept payments on Artist's behalf and deposit and distribute such payments in accordance with protocols previously agreed upon by Artist and Manager as outlined in the revocable Power of Attorney;

(b) Administrative activities to:

(1) prepare and package sample recordings and videos to submit to potential employers and booking agencies;

(2) arrange auditions and meetings;

(3) maintain all promotional supplies, organize, prepare, mail or otherwise transmit press kits and other promotional materials in support of Artist's appearances;

(4) provide general administrative support acting as a liaison with venue presenters; answering questions; solving problems and making decisions on Artist's behalf;

(5) make Artist's travel arrangements including accommodations; and

(c) Publicity-related activities to:

(1) promote and publicize Artist's name and talent including organizing promotional interviews and photo sessions and setting up local radio and television spots;

(2) supervise, approve and permit any and all publicity, press notices, public relations and advertising;

(3) with Artist's prior approval: approve and permit the use of Artist's name, likeness, voice, sound effects, caricatures, literary, artistic and musical materials for the purpose of advertising, public relations, promotion and publicity for any and all of Artist's services and in promotion and advertising of any and all products or services;

(4) with Artist's prior approval: make arrangements with packagers, bookers, sponsors, theaters, radio, television,

---

EXAMPLE 5.52

motion picture, etc. on Artist's behalf for Artist's services as well as agreements with talent or booking agencies. However, with respect to the services that are the subject of this Agreement, Artist reserves all rights and intends to retain administrative control of any and all social media accounts associated with Artist whether now in existence or to be created in the future; and

(5) with Artist's prior approval and at Artist's sole expense: engage a public relations firm to effectively present Artist's image before the public in a manner designed to further Artist's professional career.

SCOPE OF ENGAGEMENT LIMITATION CLAUSE (ARTIST MANAGER VERSION, PART B)

EXAMPLE 5.53

Artist understands and agrees that Manager is not responsible for procuring employment for Artist. Further, Artist understands that Manager is not a licensed Theatrical Talent Agent.

Note

Example 5.53 is the companion clause I referenced in the Scope of Engagement discussion, Part A. These Parts A and B tend to both be included in contracts by artist managers who work in states that regulate talent/booking agents because the manager's professional activities could be considered closer to those of an agent than those of a manager. For this reason, many managers have clauses like this one that remind artists that they are not an agent and they are not responsible for procuring employment for their artists.

Caution

Know the difference between an agent and a manager and determine whether, and to the extent that, your state regulates the activities of agents and/or managers. Why? Because you should know what recourse is available to you if you contract with an unscrupulous person or, at minimum, whether that person, if licensed, has had any complaints made against them.

Tip

At present there are several websites that can help you figure out what regulatory scheme exists, if any, in your state, but use these only as a starting point because they may not be current. State laws change. For example, Pennsylvania recently repealed the law requiring licensure and stopped regulating these professions.

Regardless of whether your manager is licensed or not, ask him whether he is a member in good standing of any professional associations. Then, contact that organization to inquire whether there have been any issues with that person's conduct. If any, ask about the details and how the issue was ultimately resolved.

Also, ask what the organization's membership screening criteria consists of (professional references, letters of good moral character, a bond, etc.); whether the association has a professional Code of Ethics that members are required to adhere to; and whether it has any continuing professional education requirements for members to remain current in their profession. In other words, do your homework.

SEVERABILITY CLAUSE

EXAMPLE 5.54

If any term or provision of this Agreement shall be determined to be illegal or unenforceable, all other terms and provisions shall remain in effect and shall be enforced to the fullest extent permitted by applicable law.

Note

Severability Clauses are important because they signal that if one portion of the contract fails for whatever reason, the remaining provisions still have effect. In other words, the entire contract will not fail just because one portion of it becomes unenforceable for some reason (the law changes or some element of it is determined to be against public policy, etc.).

EXAMPLE 5.55

The invalidity or unenforceability of any one or more terms of this Agreement shall not in any way affect the remaining terms which shall remain in full force and effect and the parties will re-negotiate in good faith a substitute provision which most nearly reflects the parties' intent in entering into this Agreement.

Note

This second example is slightly different. It provides that in the event that some language in the contract is determined to not be in compliance with the law, for whatever reason, the parties to the contract will renegotiate alternative language to replace any offending portions. Clearly, this drafter's idea is to keep the parties talking and have the contract remain in force.

Contrast a Severability Clause with a Savings Clause (Examples 5.46 and 5.47).

TERM OF ENGAGEMENT CLAUSE

EXAMPLE 5.56

Artist engages Manager as sole and exclusive agent for a term of two (2) years commencing *X* and ending *Y*.

Note

The term of engagement spells out how long the artist-management agreement will be in effect.

Caution

One or two years seems sufficient, but some of these agreements are set for much longer periods of time. There's no reason for this—you don't know what the future holds for you and whether your professional relationship with your manager will happily withstand the test of time.

Tip

If the contract you are asked to sign is longer than two years, ask for the term to be reduced to one or two years. You can always renew the agreement after this period.

Caution

Look out for other clauses that automatically renew the artist-management contract; see Renewal Clause, Example 5.42.

Caution

And as always, look for unilateral language that gives the manager the sole right to renew your contract—and be aware that it may be premised on a condition such as booking you in a Broadway show or some other longer-term venture. Maybe this isn't something you want. If you can't have the automatic renewal language removed, require that any renewals be in writing, thereby requiring a new contract. Then, at least you may be able to negotiate any objectionable terms from the old contract out of the new contract.

TERMINATION CLAUSE

EXAMPLE 5.57

Either party may terminate this Agreement with fourteen (14) days' written notice to the other party, subject to the provisions set forth in Paragraph X, Default/Notice of Cure.

Note

Not all contracts have Termination Clauses because it doesn't make sense for shorter duration contracts to have them (such as presenter contracts for a one-night engagement or a short run of shows). But expect to see them in artist-management contracts and other types of potentially longer-duration commitments like Broadway shows.

Look for ways in which the contract can be terminated. Ideally, there is a bilateral clause that gives either party the right to terminate the artist-management agreement upon X days' written notice to the other.

While Termination Clauses are beneficial to artists, they are also beneficial to managers and show producers because it allows them to get out of the contract with you too. As is the case with Example 5.57, the Termination Clause is often bundled with a Default Clause (see Example 5.16) as well as a Notice of Cure Provision.

Caution

Look out for convoluted language that attempts to circumvent the right to terminate the agreement. For example, I've seen at least one artist-management agreement that contained overlapping time periods for termination and notice of default requirements as well as strong language restricting the right to terminate the contract by creating an *agency coupled with an interest* (see Example 5.2). Remember, while managers are entitled to make an honest living and to protect their rights contractually, they are supposed to be looking out for your best interests and discharging their duties ethically.

Also look for hidden requirements that restrict the ability to terminate your contract. Example 5.58 illustrates this point.

EXAMPLE 5.58

The parties shall be entitled to terminate this Agreement upon ninety (90) days' prior written notice to the other party. Manager shall have sixty (60) days following termination to fulfill and/or finalize any commitments, obligations and/or duties commenced. Termination shall in no way affect the commission due under this Agreement.

This Agreement represents the entire understanding of the parties with respect to the subject matter hereof and may be modified, amended or terminated only by a writing signed by both parties. No waiver of any breach of this Agreement shall be construed as a continuing waiver or consent to any subsequent breach hereof.

Tip

The problem with this clause is not that the contract has a condition on termination (ninety written days' notice). The issue is twofold: (1) that termination is conditioned upon a signed writing, which is overly restrictive; and (2) that this condition is buried in a bundled clause. See Example 5.11 for a discussion of bundled clauses.

Requiring a signature to terminate a contractual relationship effectively removes the ability of one party to be able to terminate the contract, thereby defeating the underlying policy and purpose of having a Termination Clause at all.

Let's say you wanted to terminate your contractual relationship and you had this type of signature requirement. If you gave your manager (or producer) proper notice of your intention to terminate the agreement, this signature requirement would condition the termination on the other party's willingness to allow the termination. This is far too restrictive.

This is another example of the importance of reading and understanding every clause in any contract you sign.

TERRITORY CLAUSE

EXAMPLE 5.59

The territory of this Agreement shall be the world.

Note

The Territory Clause defines the geographic territory for where the authority given to your manager via the Agency Clause (Example 5.1) and narrowed by the Scope of Engagement Clause (Example 5.49) applies.

Tip

It's proper to limit the geographic territory of the manager's authority to only those territories where the manager can actually work for you. It's common for American classical musicians under management to have a manager in the United States (with authority in the United States, its territories and possessions, and Canada) as well as another manager in Europe.

WAIVER CLAUSE

EXAMPLE 5.60

Failure of [union], the artist or the employer to insist upon the strict enforcement of any of the provisions of this Agreement shall not be deemed a waiver of any rights or remedies that [union] may have and shall not be deemed a waiver of any subsequent breach or default on the part of the employer, the artist or [union].

Note

A Waiver Clause allows for a deviation from one or more of the conditions or restrictions in a contract. In other words, waivers permit something that the contract, on its face, does not allow. Waiver Clauses are generally written to say that the allowance of one deviation from what the contract requires doesn't mean that others will be allowed as well.

In other words, it says, "Just because I allowed it once doesn't mean that: (1) I sanctioned it, (2) you can do it again, or (3) someone else may do the same thing just because you did."

Distinguish an Amendment Clause (Example 5.4) from a Waiver Clause. An amendment is a change to the contract that is typically intended to remain in effect for the balance of the agreement. A waiver is an agreement not to enforce a particular term in a particular instance.

WORK-FOR-HIRE CLAUSE

EXAMPLE 5.61

Works for Hire belong to the hiring entity the same way that a pharmaceutical company owns the intellectual property developed by its scientists. Musicians, particularly songwriters and composers, who create things for others for a fee/commission need to be careful about protecting their creations. In order to retain the copyright to the works they create, the contract should have a clause stating that the musician retains ownership of the creation (if that's the intent) and that it is not a "work for hire."

WORK PRODUCT CLAUSE

EXAMPLE 5.62

It is hereby agreed that any material whatsoever, including any form of "stage business" performed by Actor in rehearsals or any performance of the Play, shall, insofar as Actor is concerned, be the property of Producer and/or the Authors of the Play, as their respective interests may appear.

Note

Work Product Clauses are common in many types of employment contracts. They are important because many employees/independent contractors don't realize that the product(s) that result from their work efforts (whether a character in a play, an invention, or a laboratory method) legally belong to the employer and not to the person who literally created it.

In the context of a television show, for example, if your small walk-on role has the potential to become its own spin-off show, that character, though created by you, belongs to the show's producers. If you were interested in developing it as a spin-off, you would need to secure the rights to it from the originating show's producers.

6

A Step-by-Step Guide for Analyzing Your Contracts

If you've read Chapter 4, you now have some things to look for along the way, so let's go.

You have been given a contract to sign and it's time to figure out what it says *before you sign it*—because the law presumes that if you've signed it, you understand its terms and agree to all of them.

The following step-by-step plan will make it easier for you to understand what the contract says and how the interplay between the individual clauses works.

You can develop your own strategy, of course—you may prefer to do all your analysis electronically using your computer's software program—but this is the strategy I use.

STEP I: PREPPING THE CONTRACT

1. **Make a copy.** If you have an electronic file of the contract, print a copy out to mark up. If you only have a hard copy, ask for an electronic copy (even if it is locked) so you can use your computer's software program to help with your review. Or just make a second (working) copy to mark up.
2. **Is it complete?** Review the contract to determine that it is complete, with no missing pages. Are any addendums referenced? If so, are they all there?

3. **Ready?** Once you're sure that everything is accounted for, you're ready to get to work. You will be reading the contract several times with different purposes in mind to cull out the essential details.

4. **Add identifying markers.** Identifying markers will make it easier to read when any items are cross-referenced within the contract, such as a word that is used in one section but defined in another section.

   ▪ Make sure that every section (if divided up into sections) has some marker; give it either a capital letter or Roman numeral if no other marker is used.

   ▪ Check each section to make certain that every clause or paragraph within each section is numbered. If no numbers are used, assign each clause a number. For example, if there is a section of defined terms, give each term a number or letter if none has been provided.

   As noted in Chapter 4, whenever a term is defined in a contract, its meaning is being narrowed. The drafter is intending to limit the term's meaning specifically to that definition rather than the term's commonly understood meaning (or some other interpretation).

STEP II: SETTING UP THE ROADMAP

At this point, some people prefer to read the definitions, if any, so that they can keep *defined terms* in mind as they read through the contract. If there aren't many definitions or if the definitions are simple, that approach is fine. But, in some contracts, a defined term can be a paragraph's length of words separated by commas. In that case, don't rely on your memory; instead follow my approach.

1. Starting at the top of the contract, you are going to use specific markings in the left margin to provide you with a framework for navigating through the contract now that every section and clause has an identifying marker:

   ▪ Use a check mark (√) to indicate that you've read and understand a given clause or paragraph and don't need to circle back to it right away. You will reread it later, after all the marking up.

   ▪ Use a Q to indicate a question—you don't understand the clause or have some issue you want clarified.

   ▪ Mark any clause or defined term that is cross-referenced within the contract with a corresponding number or letter above it each time it appears.

For example, if *gross income* is the fourth defined term in the contract, each time that term appears, you should place a *4* above it so you can easily flip to it when you read the sentence again later.

2. If the contract uses *recitals*, read each recital to be sure that it is an accurate reflection of the contract's background. Remember that the purpose of the recitals section is to provide some context about you, the other party, the nature of the contract itself, and the nature of your relationship to the other party for the benefit of third-party readers who may need to interpret the contract without knowing anything about it. Place a check mark (√) or a Q next to each recital item as applicable; see Chapter 4 for a discussion of contract recitals.

3. Go back to the top. This time you will look for limiting or broadening language. Underline limiting language and circle broadening language. Usually where such language appears, at least one party's rights are being truncated at the expense of the other party's rights; see Chapter 4.

Example of limiting language: Manager has the *sole* right to renew this contract.

4. Go back again, but this time look for *unilateral* clauses and underline them; circle *bilateral* clauses; see Chapter 4. Don't worry yet about which party these clauses benefit; you'll get to that a little later.

5. Now search the document for any uses of *defined terms* being used in their undefined sense, because when a term is defined, it means only the definition given; when it's not defined, it means something that is broader than the meaning given. If you do see dual usages, don't assume that it's due to sloppy drafting—it could be an intentional treatment. You should know what is intended. Defined terms usually appear in bold, caps, italics, or some combination of these.

STEP III: ANALYZING THE CONTRACT

At this point, every clause and defined term should have a corresponding number (or letter) and every time each appears in the contract, it should have its number (or letter) above it. This will provide a roadmap for your analysis because you will be bouncing from section to section and will need to keep a lot of information at your fingertips.

1. **Just read.** Now I recommend that you read the contract straight through and let it sink in a bit. Then go do something else, if time permits, and come back to the contract later with a fresh set of eyes.

2. **Read and mark.** You're back and you're rested. Now that you're back at it, take your time and read each clause slowly once more. Wherever a clause or term is cross-referenced, go to it and read it within the context of the clause where it is embedded. If you've put a check mark (√) in the margin and it still makes sense, you're done with that item. For any items indicated with a Q, you are going to make a list for following up later.

   Some issues indicated with a Q might be:
   a. You don't understand the clause or its function.
   b. The clause seems out of place to you (i.e., it does not belong in this type of contract).
   c. The clause seems unfair to you in some way (e.g., it's unilateral, giving broader rights to the other party than to you).
   d. The clause doesn't accurately reflect the agreement as you understood it.

3. **Analyze defined terms.** Again, if your contract uses *defined terms*, but periodically you see those words being used in their *undefined* sense (i.e., not shown in bold, caps, or quotes), don't assume it's a mistake because it could be intentional. It could mean that the term is intended to be interpreted more broadly in those instances than when it appears in its defined sense. Conversely, if the defined term is not sufficient for the context, but is acceptable in the general usage, take note of those instances.

   Which interpretation makes sense to you? Read the clause both ways and if you think it's important enough for clarification, get the issue clarified in writing or have the correction made by the other party.

4. **Critically read.** Now, go back and reread each clause that is underlined or circled to determine whether the language used makes sense to you. For example, circled items (which you've just identified as being *bilateral*), indicate a plus (+) for clauses that you approve or a minus (-) for those clauses that restrict your rights in a way that you do not approve.

5. **Make a list.** Now, make a list of all the items indicated with a Q in the margin and all clauses with a minus (-) that indicate that your rights are being reduced in some way. This list contains all the items that you want clarified or changed.

6. **Catalog missing elements.** Finally, does the contract contain every detail that was negotiated/discussed? In other words, were there any promises made to you or by you that are not contained within the contract? If anything is missing, you will need to get it included within the contract before signing it. If later you discover that an important issue or something important is missing and an amendment is not possible, another option is to have a completely different contract drawn up only for that missing item.

   Remember, if something important is missing from the contract, you may have a difficult time later proving that it was part of the deal (see the discussion on the operation of the Merger Clause in Chapter 5).

STEP IV: RESPONDING

1. If you have questions or issues you'd like clarified, put them in writing and send them to the other party for clarification. If you send your questions via e-mail, but get a phone call or some other non-written response in return, take good notes; if you are satisfied with the response, ask when you can expect a revised contract to sign if that's the result you are looking for. If you are told not to worry ("Just sign and return"), then you must decide whether it's worth the risk. But take good notes of all conversations and date your entries.

2. If you do get another, written version of the contract back but it has not been corrected, correct it yourself and provide your initials next to each correction. Send it back for the other party to sign or amend.

3. Sign the contract only if it contains all the items you agreed to and if all the issues or questions raised have been settled to your satisfaction. Keep in mind: paying attention to detail and looking out for your interests is not "being difficult"; it's being a good businessperson.

STEP V: REVIEWING

1. Once you have a final contract that is an accurate reflection of the deal, sign and return it, in the manner specified. If it's a presenter's contract and you feel that it's important enough to have an attorney review it prior to signing, then engage an attorney who is familiar with the customs of contracts of this type (opera, theater, composition, etc.).

2. If it's an artist-management contract, I encourage you to engage an attorney or another experienced person to review it because those types of

contracts can have very long lives and, as such, can bind you well into the future, long after the contractual relationship is over. An example of this is if your manager books you into a long-running Broadway show (or, if you are an artist who works in popular music, you sign a record deal) and you subsequently decide to sever the relationship with the manager. He may have an ongoing right to a percentage of your earnings for the duration of your tenure in that show (or to earnings from the record); see Chapter 9.

STEP VI: RECORDKEEPING

1. **Scan/name it.** Once you have a final copy of your contract with all the required signatures, scan it using a name that make sense to you and keep it in an electronic folder for future access. Or if you prefer to maintain hard copies, file your contracts, but organize and keep them somewhere safe.
2. **File it.** Maintain a file for your artist-management contract that contains all correspondences that are specific to that relationship, including letters, e-mails, and any handwritten notes you took from phone calls or other conversations.
3. **File it.** Maintain separate files for all your engagement contracts as well, by presenter and calendar year, including letters, e-mails, and any handwritten notes you took from phone calls or other conversations.
4. **Bring it with you.** Bring a copy of your presenters' contracts to your gigs in case you need to reference them. I had a client who was in the chorus of a Broadway show. The cast traveled to California to record the album. Very late one night she called me for advice, telling me that the chorus, convinced that the wrong union's wage calculations were being used to determine their payment for the recording, was planning to boycott further work on the album. I asked her what the contract said about recordings and wage disputes. In a room of experienced musicians, not one of them had brought the contract with them to this gig.
5. **Retain it.** Most tax professionals suggest keeping documents like these for at least seven years in case you are audited by the IRS.
6. **Keep notes.** If a dispute arises under any of your contracts, keep detailed notes of each person you speak with, when you spoke, and what was said. Chapter 9 provides some guidance for handling disputes and recordkeeping.

Part III

PERFORMERS' CONTRACTS

7

Musician's Engagement (Gig) Contracts

There are all kinds of contracts that serve all kinds of purposes. Before we can discuss the specifics of performers' contracts, you will need to know how they differ from other services contracts, what clauses the contracts should contain, and why. The two basic types of services contracts are *general services contracts* and *personal services contracts*.

GENERAL SERVICES CONTRACTS

A *general services contract* is one in which you hire services to be performed, but *not* a specific person to perform them. Consider the example of buying new kitchen cabinets for installation at a big-box store. In this example, you are purchasing both *goods* and *services*: the cabinets are the goods and the installation of the cabinets is the service. When you engage the store to install the cabinets, the service is a *general services contract* because you are not hiring someone specific to do the installation. In reality, you hire the store and the store subcontracts this work out (delegates its contractual duty) to a local contractor who, presumably, has been fully vetted by the store and is qualified to perform the services contracted. When the store subcontracts out this work, it is responsible (legally liable) to you for the quality of the contractor's work. If it is subpar, the store may take action against the contractor according to its contract with him. In legal terms, you and the store have *privity of contract*. The contractor is likely an independent contractor in *privity* with the store.

PERSONAL SERVICES CONTRACTS

By contrast, a *personal services contract*, such as a musician's contract to perform, is one where the person doing the hiring is engaging a specific person. Because each musician's gifts are considered unique to that individual, a musician contracted to perform may not hire out another musician to take his place (delegate his contractual duties) unless the contract allows it, but these contracts usually do not.

The policy behind this restriction is that *personal services contracts* are, well, *personal* in nature. If you are hired for a gig, the person hiring you is legally entitled to your musicianship and talents, not someone else's regardless of how qualified the other musician may be. Generally, you cannot subcontract (delegate) your contractual obligations to a third party without the hiring person's consent.

PERSONAL SERVICES CONTRACTS: THE BASICS

Just as a contract for the sale of goods will contain the clauses necessary to complete the sale (a description of the goods, quantity, quality requirements, price, date, and manner of delivery and a warranty of the goods' utility for a specific purpose, etc.), a *personal services contract* will contain all the clauses necessary for the services to be performed (when, how, and when payment for those services should be made).

Personal services contracts will, of course, differ by type and industry, but they generally contain the following concepts:

- a clause spelling out the specific services to be performed
- a deadline for completion (possibly with milestone due dates for progress payments)
- permissible expenses and a budget for costs
- payment details (per project or hourly basis)
- any invoicing or reporting requirements
- duration of the contract if not terminated early
- representations of the service provider regarding his qualifications to perform the services in compliance with the law (licensing)
- any details specific to the parties
- materiality, breach, and termination details, including Default and Notice of Cure Provisions

TWO TYPES OF MUSICIANS' ENGAGEMENT (GIG) CONTRACTS

Musicians' *personal services contracts* with presenters are called *engagement (gig) contracts*. These are the contracts used by presenters to hire musicians to perform.

Presenters' engagement contracts come in two general varieties: (1) pre-negotiated union versions; and (2) non-union versions designed by the presenter themselves—often by a law firm engaged to create standardized ("boilerplate") language for that organization.

PRE-NEGOTIATED UNION CONTRACTS

Union contracts have presumably been prepared with artists' best interests in mind by the union representatives who negotiated the Collective Bargaining Agreement (CBA) between the union and the presenter. A CBA is contract between a presenter/employer and its union member. It contains the regulations and conditions of employment.

For example, the Metropolitan Opera, being a presenter of operas, is an American Guild of Musical Artists (AGMA) signatory company. This means that the people who sing or dance in opera productions at the Met are members of AGMA and that AGMA has negotiated the essential terms of employment for its members/artists.

While the CBA contains the general terms governing an engagement, artists will also have a *standard artists' contract* and any applicable riders, which will outline specifics such as the artist's fee, rehearsal and performance dates, role, etc. Because the terms of these contracts have (presumably) been negotiated in good faith by the employer and union representatives, they are, in large part, not negotiable by artists and so not discussed here.

NON-UNION ENGAGEMENT CONTRACTS

The other type of *personal services contracts* are non-union *engagement contracts*. These contracts will contain many of the common clauses discussed in Chapter 5, but also anything else that is important to that organization and to your appearance. Minimally, you should expect to see all of the basics relating specifically to your engagement with that presenter:

- what you will be performing
- performance venue
- performance date and time
- what fee will be paid

Recall from Chapter 2 that all valid contracts contain duties, rights, and often restrictions for all of the parties to the contract. Be certain that your contract contains enough of the key details required for it to be valid. To do this, be sure your engagement (gig) contract contains all the details indicated above, or you risk not being able to have anything to enforce if your appearance is canceled.

Beyond the essential basic terms required for a valid contract, there may be more favorable terms you'd prefer to see in your engagement contract. Negotiating non-essential terms of non-union house contracts is possible, but not easy because of the volume of contracts these entities enter into annually. Typically, they have developed boilerplate language with their attorneys, and that is the model they use repeatedly. However, if you have an objection to language used in one or more of the clauses you see, ask for the language to be modified. Suggest some alternate language. It can't hurt to ask.

What follows is an example of a classical musician's recital contract. Each clause is annotated with an explanation, in italics, of what it does. You will recognize some of the clauses from Chapter 5.

Chapter 8 contains an overview of agents and managers and includes an annotated artist-management contract. If you're interested in content typical of a producer agreement, the annotated artist-management contract contains several examples of what you'd likely see in that type of arrangement.

I don't provide any content specific to a recording contract for the following reasons: recording contracts are rare and very complicated, and I've never negotiated or drafted one. More important, while I want to empower you to read and understand all of the content in your contracts, I don't want to lead you to believe that you can negotiate a recording contract on your own. The stakes are too high and the royalty accounting clauses too perilous. If you are lucky enough to get a record deal, engage an entertainment lawyer (who is not also your manager) to negotiate it for you.

AN ANNOTATED PRESENTER'S ENGAGEMENT CONTRACT

WHEREAS Artist is a _____.

WHEREAS _____ is Artist's Manager.

WHEREAS Presenter is a non-for-profit organization whose primary business is presenting live musical or other artistic or creative acts to the public for an admission fee.

WHEREAS Presenter acknowledges that *X* is Artist's authorized agent for the purposes of contractually binding Artist to perform at Presenter's venue (Engagement).

These "whereas" clauses are called recitals. Considered by some to be old-fashioned, recitals serve an important function in a contract: they provide some context and background for third-party readers like judges and arbitrators by providing insight into the purpose of the contract. There will often be a title page that precedes this boilerplate document. The title page will often outline the details specific to the artist's performance(s), including the program name, if any; the place(s), time(s), and date(s) of the performances; the artist's fee; and any other financial considerations such as fee advances, per diems, and travel and/or housing allowances.

The parties mutually agree as follows:

This is the Mutuality Provision; see Chapter 2, Offer and Acceptance.

1. Presenter will pay Artist's fee in full within 48 hours of the engagement.

   This clause sets out some of the necessary housekeeping provisions. Payment of the artist's engagement fee can be made to the artist directly or to the artist's manager (if he has one), based on their arrangement.

2. If Artist is unable to perform the Engagement for any reason beyond the control of the Artist, including without limitation, illness of the Artist or death or life-threatening illness of an immediate family member of Artist, accident, or any incapacity, fires, labor disputes or Acts of God ("force majeure"), this Agreement shall terminate with respect to the Engagement and neither party shall be liable to the other for damages arising out of the Artist's inability to perform. If, for any reasons, Artist is able to perform only a portion of the Engagement, then the Engagement fee

shall be reduced pro-rata.[1] Cancellation or rescheduling by Presenter due to Presenter's fiscal insolvency, poor ticket sales or scheduling problems, or for any other reason, shall not be deemed a force majeure event giving rise to termination without liability on the part of the Presenter;

This is an expanded version of a Force Majeure Clause. For a discussion of force majeure and a definition of damages, see Chapter 5. The last sentence indicating that the presenter's financial problems or poor ticket sales won't excuse a breach of contract is a benefit for the artist and is what the law requires. This means that the presenter cannot cancel the engagement without paying the artist's fee. Unfortunately, some unscrupulous presenters have used the Force Majeure Clause to try to avoid following what the law requires when they had to cancel a production due to budget problems. Read the story about the stage director in the preface for one such example.

3. Presenter will provide: (1) the performance site and rehearsal area, including stage and dressing room, furniture, stage lighting, sound equipment and other items, each as reasonably requested by Artist and each in clean, comfortable and safe condition; (2) personnel to operate all such equipment, all necessary house staff (back and front house), and a page turner (if requested by Artist), each at Presenter's expense; and (3) Presenter further agrees to honor Artist's specific needs as detailed in any riders attached hereto;

This clause lays out two important things: (1) the basic requirements for the artist's appearance, and (2) that the artist will not need to hire out or otherwise pay for these necessities.

4. Presenter agrees to include text and/or inserts as provided by Artist (through Manager) in each program and program credits as follows: _____;

5. Presenter will use best efforts to provide the requests stipulated in any rider attached hereto;

The rider, referenced here and in several other places throughout this contract, will contain specific requirements by the artist in support of the artist's appearance. For example, it may require a certain number of complimentary tickets, bottled water, or even a first-floor dressing room because the artist has difficulty with stairs.

6. Neither the performance nor rehearsals shall be broadcast, filmed, photographed, recorded, televised, videotaped, or otherwise reproduced or extended beyond the Engagement site without prior written consent of Artist, through Artist's Manager;

   This is good for the artist because she may want to control how her image is being represented and, ultimately, would want to be compensated if recording, etc., were allowed.

7. If requested, and at Presenter's sole expense, Presenter will supply the following equipment required for Artist's engagement: _____ _____;

8. Presenter will be solely responsible for payment of all license fees or royalties required in connection with performance of works on the program;

   This clause makes the presenter responsible for obtaining rights clearances and for paying royalties for licensed material that the artist uses in the performance.

9. Presenter will produce the program for the Engagement at its own expense. If requested, Presenter agrees to supply Artist, through Manager, with all pages of the program on which Artist's name or likeness appears and such pages are subject to Artist's approval, through Manager;

   This is a Credits Clause. The manager will likely want to approve how credits are given. Further, the artist may be contractually obligated to show those credits in a specific way. For example, "Artist appears courtesy of RCA Records."

10. This Agreement, including any riders attached hereto, may not be modified without the other party's prior written consent;

*This is an Amendment Clause (specifically, a restriction against making any
unilateral changes to the contract); see Chapter 5.*

11. Presenter agrees to defend, indemnify and hold Artist, its officers, employees and agents harmless from and against any and all liability, loss,
expense (including reasonable attorney's fees) or claims for injuries or
damages arising out of the performance of this Agreement but only in
proportion and to the extent such liability, loss, expense, attorney's fees
or claims for injury or damages are caused by or result from the negligent or intentional acts or omissions of Presenter, its officers, agents
or employees;

See the comments under item 12.

12. Artist agrees to defend, indemnify and hold Presenter, its officers, employees and agents harmless from and against any and all liability, loss,
expense (including reasonable attorney's fees) or claims for injury or
damages arising out of the performance of this Agreement but only in
proportion to and to the extent such liability, loss, expense, attorney's fees
or claims for injury or damages are caused by or result from the negligent
or intentional acts or omissions of Artist, its officers, agents, or employees;

*Clauses 11 and 12 are bilateral Indemnification Clauses. They mirror one
another so that each party has made the same contractual promises to the
other with respect to indemnification. Recall that Indemnification Clauses
contain two promises: (1) to defend (hire legal counsel), and (2) to indemnify (pay the court-ordered damages if you lose the lawsuit).*

*Consider the following hypothetical situation on how this clause could be
invoked: The presenter has agreed, via item 8 of this sample contract, to
secure licensing and pay royalties for material that the artist will use in
his performance. The artist decides to change some of the recital material
without telling the presenter. No rights are granted for the use of the new*

material because no royalties are paid for it. After the performance, artist and presenter are both sued for copyright infringement for using protected material without the content owner's permission.

In the hypothetical, the artist has committed to: (1) hiring an attorney to represent both himself and the presenter in the lawsuit (defend); and (2) if the plaintiff's copyright infringement suit is successful against the artist and the presenter, paying the full judgment rendered against both of them, including the presenter's share of liability, if any (indemnify the presenter).

Ideally, these clauses wouldn't exist because it is entirely possible that if something does go wrong and liability is assessed against the artist and presenter, the cost of the defense and indemnity could easily exceed the value of the contract by many multiples.

13. Should Presenter incur any claims, damages, other liabilities or costs and expenses relating to the non-appearance of Artist for reasons other than those enumerated above in connection with the Engagement, Artist's liability shall not exceed fifteen percent (15%) of Artist's fee hereunder;

This seems very reasonable to me. Depending on when the artist cancels the engagement, the presenter likely will have laid out money in support of the artist's appearance. Those costs (many of which are enumerated within this contract) should be known to the artist. The 15% maximum is a generous limitation on what could be a substantial outlay of costs associated with printing programs, tickets, and marketing collateral; preparing press releases; and setting up e-tickets and television and newspaper ads, etc.

14. This Agreement is governed by and construed in accordance with the laws of the State of New York, without giving effect to the principles of conflicts thereof. In the event a dispute arises under this Agreement which cannot be resolved, such dispute shall be submitted to arbitration and resolved by a single arbitrator (who shall be a lawyer) in accordance with the Commercial Arbitration rules of the American Arbitration Association (AAA) then in effect.

All such arbitration shall take place at the office of the (AAA) located in New York, NY. Each party is entitled to depose one (1) fact witness and any expert retained by the other party, and to conduct such other discovery[2] as the arbitrator deems appropriate. The arbitration provisions of this Agreement shall not prevent any party from obtaining injunctive relief from a court of competent jurisdiction to enforce the obligations for which such party may obtain provisional relief pending a decision on the merits[3] by an arbitrator. Each of the parties hereby consents to the jurisdiction of New York courts for such purpose. The award or decision rendered by the arbitrator shall be final, binding and conclusive. Judgment may be entered upon such award by any court;

This is a bundled clause combining a Choice of Law Provision and an Arbitration Provision; see Chapter 5 for a discussion of each of these. See Chapter 3 for a discussion of injunction as a breach of contract remedy.

The phrase without giving effect to the principles of conflicts *operates as follows: where the governing law is contested or is otherwise in question, states have legal tests they invoke in order to determine which law should apply based on the facts and the area of law at issue. This phrase says that despite the availability of conflict of law tests, New York State law will supersede that analysis and govern the terms of this arrangement.*

15. This Agreement cannot be assigned without prior written consent of Artist, through Manager;

This is an Assignment Clause. These are very common in musicians' contracts because of the very personal nature of what musicians and other creative people do. The other party, in this case a presenter, includes this clause so that the artist doesn't subcontract her performing duties to another musician; see Chapter 5.

16. All rights and remedies of the parties under this Agreement are cumulative and not in limitation or restriction of any other right or remedy in law or in equity; and

This is a Remedies Clause; see Chapters 3 and 5. It says that if either party has a dispute with the other regarding the other's performance or non-performance under the contract, each could seek monetary damages (a remedy "in law") and/or another, non-monetary remedy (one "in equity") such as an injunction.

17. This Agreement contains the entire agreement between the parties and shall supersede all prior proposals, negotiations, agreements, arrangements and understandings, if any, relating to the obligations and matters set out herein, whether oral or written.

This is a Merger Clause. Merger Clauses say that all the promises both parties made to each other during the negotiation process (which is assumed) are contained in the contract. These clauses are powerful because they indicate to a judge that a specific rule of evidence applies that will prohibit the judge from hearing and viewing any evidence (even if written) that contradicts terms within the contract; see Chapter 5.

_____	_____
Artist	Date

_____	_____
On behalf of Presenter	Date

8

Personal Representation

There has been long-standing confusion concerning what the various titles mean within the context of artist representation. The following titles depend on the individual's role in supporting an artist's career. Here is a breakdown of the various titles in this industry, all of which fall under the broad umbrella of "personal representative":

Agent	*Manager*
Booking Agent	Business Manager
Talent Agent	Personal Manager
	Publicity Manager
	Road Manager
	Artist Manager

AGENT OR MANAGER: "HAVE YOUR PEOPLE CALL MY PEOPLE"

Despite our casual approach to referring to these professionals, there is an important distinction to be made between agents and managers: an *agent's* primary responsibility is to procure employment for an artist; a *personal manager's* primary responsibility is, very broadly, to guide an artist's career.

For more information about agents and the distinction between agents and managers, read the chapter on this subject in Krasilovsky and Shemel's *This Business of Music*.[1] The Krasilovsky book provides details specific to New York and California—the two states that have taken the most proactive approaches to regulating those who manage talent.

AGENT

The terms *booking agent* and *talent agent* are used by many people interchangeably. The terms may have state-specific distinctions, but in essence, an agent's job is to "create opportunities, procure and negotiate employment for clients and counsel them in the development of their careers."[2] Artists (and groups) within the popular music industry often have agents who book them into performance venues. These artists often employ both agents and managers. Artists in the theatrical space may have an agent (called a "theatrical talent agent" in New York) who books gigs for them or who gets them auditions for gigs. They may also have a manager. Classical musicians typically don't have agents; they only have managers.

I don't include analysis of a licensed agent's contract here because artists who hire those professionals already have state oversight on their side because their agent's contracts are uniform, state-approved documents with required content designed to protect artists' interests.

Regulating Agents

Just as they do for lawyers, physicians, real estate agents, and so many other professions, states regulate agents through licensure. However, there is no uniform approach across state lines. Some states have no licensing mechanism at all; some merely require agents to have a business license; others, like California and New York, have elaborate statutes that regulate the activities of agents.

The states that do proactively regulate agents tend to license them as they do employment agencies.[3] California's Talent Agencies Act requires that those who book jobs for talent have an agency license issued by the California Department of Labor. However, the law provides an exception for professionals whose responsibility it is to seek a record contract for talent. While there is no criminal penalty for acting as an agent without a license in California, the labor commissioner has disgorged profits (commissions) from those who have acted as an agent without a license.

New York State licenses talent agencies under New York General Business Law (GBL). New York talent agencies located outside of New York City are licensed and regulated by the New York State Department of Labor in Albany. Talent agencies located within New York City are licensed and regulated by the New York City Department of Consumer Affairs and must comply with the city's Cultural Affairs Law as well as with the GBL. Regardless of the agency's location, licensure requirements include strict recordkeeping practices; restrictions on fee structures (including a cap on agent commissions); and requirements regarding contract content with artists, advertising practices, and the types and locations of professional services they can provide. In New York State it is a crime to act as an unlicensed agent.[4]

Many musicians are members of unions whose role it is to safeguard talent against abuses of presenters. Some unions also indirectly regulate the agents who represent artists. The American Federation of Musicians (AFM), American Federation of Television and Radio Artists (AFTRA), and American Guild of Variety Artists (AGVA) require their members to work with agents who have union franchise certificates. This requirement protects artists because the unions set the contract terms such as fees, commissions, and work hours.

Professional Associations for Agents

Talent agent can be a generic term used to refer to a licensed agent, but it can also specifically refer to an agent who is a member of the Association of Talent Agents (ATA) based in Los Angeles.[5] This association and its strategic partner, the New York National Association of Talent Representatives, are not talent agencies themselves; they are non-profit trade associations for licensed agents that provide professional development, create networking opportunities, and establish best practices, including an ethical code of conduct and lobbying efforts for their industry.

Why This Is Important

Like any profession, there are good agents and bad agents, principled and unscrupulous. Having a regulatory framework in place protects artists from being taken advantage of by providing an opportunity to report abuses and encourages uniformity within the state with respect to some key issues such as agent contract content, fee structures, and other safeguards. And it's generally considered a good idea for those who engage an agent (or manager for that matter) to find one who is a member of a professional association because such membership often involves some form of professional credentials vetting, adherence to professional standards of conduct and best practices guidelines, and the organization's member-developed code of ethics.

MANAGERS

The term *manager* generally encompasses the synonymous terms *personal manager* (as used in California) and *artist manager* (as used in New York). As noted above, the primary role of a manager is to design and guide the arc of an artist's career as well as handle the daily responsibilities of supporting the artist's engagements. In California, personal managers can also shop for record deals for their clients, but cannot book engagements for artists without an agency license. To avoid confusion, I will use the generic term *artist manager* going forward to refer to professionals who manage and guide artists' careers.

Other types of managers are business managers, publicity managers, and road managers. Their functions can be broken down as follows:

- Business managers are generally accountants or tax attorneys who handle the financial aspect of an artist's career. They may collect artist contract fees, write checks on the artist's behalf, and pay all the people who work for the artist as well as provide financial planning advice.
- Publicity managers, in conjunction with an artist's manager, provide publicity and media support for the artist's engagements.
- Road managers handle the daily aspects of an artist's tour.

Business managers, publicity managers, and road managers are common for popular music artists, but much less so for classical and theatrical musicians.

Regulating Managers

Managers are rarely licensed, presumably because their primary function is not to procure employment for artists. As noted above, artist managers are responsible for guiding artists' careers. That's the official line. In reality, managers are also expected to use their professional expertise and connections to find work for the artists on their roster. This, after all, is where the money comes from, so that the artists can pay the managers their commissions.

At this point you may be wondering how managers can seek employment for their artists without an agency license. Great question! In states where there is no licensing scheme, there's no problem, but in others it's tricky. In California, as noted above, there is an exception to licensure for those who are shopping for record deals for their clients, but the statute doesn't specifically provide an exception from licensure for managers. In New York, there is an exception to licensure. New York draws a distinction between theatrical talent agents and artist managers. In New York, agents are required to be licensed because their primary business is the procurement of employment for those they represent. Managers, on the other hand, operate under an exception to the licensing requirement because the procurement of employment for their artists is only "incidental" to the overall catalog of services that they provide. California and New York, being such important cultural centers in the United States, have the most robust regulatory schemes in place for the protection of artists.

Considering all the requirements on agents, particularly the cap on commissions, it should be no surprise that an artist representative would elect to identify as an artist manager under New York law—responsible for guiding and advising artists, rather than committing to the primary business function of procuring employment for artists. For this reason, you will commonly see language in artist-management contracts that spells out all the manager's responsibilities in great detail as well as a companion clause that states that the manager is not responsible for procuring employment for the artist.

So, the term *artist manager* is a generic one used to refer to people in the business of counseling and promoting the careers of creative people—whether they are musicians, actors, writers, directors, visual artists, or artists of another kind—and these professionals are rarely required to be licensed.

Professional Associations for Managers

Like agents, managers also have professional trade associations. Two prominent ones are the National Conference of Personal Managers (NCOPM) and the North American Performing Arts Managers and Agents (NAPAMA). NAPAMA membership, as its name suggests, includes agents.

NCOPM says that a personal manager is a professional with expertise "to find and develop new talent, advise and counsel talent, and act as a liaison between their clients and talent agents, publicists, attorneys, business managers, and other entertainment industry personnel."[6]

NAPAMA's mission statement is "to promote the best interests of performing arts agents and managers through leadership, professional development and alliances in the performing arts industry."[7]

Artist-Management Contracts

Keep in mind that all contracts are negotiable. In addition to being an artist, you are also a businessperson. You are the CEO of your own business and you are in the best position to protect your interests—do not give that power to anyone who could potentially have a conflict of interest in this regard. They may well be ardent admirers of what you do, but in the end, your job is to make money for them. It's a business relationship.

If there is no room for negotiating the terms of an artist-management contract, then move on to someone who will be a more equal business partner. If one person sees your potential, then it is very likely that another will as well.

Consider hiring an attorney (or other experienced professional) to review any artist-management agreement that you are asked to sign. The person does not need to be an entertainment lawyer; he or she only needs to understand what you do for a living and what is standard in that industry. If you do hire an attorney and decide to request some changes to the contract, which is well within your rights, ask to be present during the negotiations. Listen and learn—you are paying for the work, after all.

Over time you will develop confidence to handle these and other business matters, and it will be second nature to you to put your CEO hat on periodically. With practice, you will become a fierce advocate for your artist-self.

You know from Chapter 7 that *personal services contracts* are fairly uniform because they have certain required clauses that are necessary in order to make the arrangement work as intended. Artist-management contracts work the same way: there are several clauses that are essential for the manager to effectively represent an artist. These clauses give rights to the manager to conduct business on your behalf. The danger, of course, in any situation where you give authority to another to act on your behalf, is giving away too much authority and/or not retaining control over how that authority is exercised.

GIVING UP CONTROL—A DELICATE BALANCING ACT

Before I introduce common artist-management contract clauses in detail, consider how much control you want to retain over the day-to-day management of your career and what you are comfortable giving up to your manager.

There are many ways to give or relinquish control under a contract. In an artist-management contract, each artist must decide for himself what the right balance is between retaining too much control and giving up too much control.

Consider what is most important to you, including use of your likeness/ image, performance venues, music genres, length of engagements/time away from home, type of travel and accommodations, and performance fees. You can contractually limit how much control to give to your manager over such issues as follows:

a. by subjecting the manager's decisions to your prior approval;
b. by subjecting the manager's decisions to your prior *written* approval;
c. by putting dollar amount caps/length limitations/venue restrictions/etc. on gigs that your manager can bind you to without your express consent;
d. by requiring that the use of your photograph/caricature/image/etc. be approved by you if distribution will be over a predetermined length of time or outside a designated geographic area; and so on.

Before you get too restrictive, though, keep in mind that you and your manager are supposed to be working together toward the same ends. The more you restrict his or her ability to effectively promote you and advance your career, the more difficult it will be for that goal to be met.

THE MECHANICS OF AN ARTIST-MANAGEMENT CONTRACT

The essential elements of an artist-management contract can be divided into four general categories that are necessary for bringing the contractual relationship to life. These categories provide a framework for all the content that follows. The four categories are:

1. clauses relating to the transfer of rights
2. financial clauses
3. clauses relating to timing
4. housekeeping clauses

Clauses Relating to the Transfer of Rights

Contract clauses relating to the transfer of rights are the:

- Agency Clause—artist gives manager the right to do things on artist's behalf
- Scope of Engagement Clause—lists the services and responsibilities that the manager is taking on for the artist

- Exclusivity Clause—restricts artist from similarly engaging another manager
- Non-exclusivity Clause—states that manager provides similar services to other artists
- Partnership Clause—spells out that the nature of the agreement does not rise to the level of being a partnership between artist and manager; sometimes clarifies that manager is an independent contractor, not artist's employee
- Power of Attorney Clause—outlines the legal rights being transferred by artist to manager and/or commits artist to granting such powers via another document such as a standardized, state-specific Power of Attorney form, where applicable
- Assignment Clause—gives the manager the right to delegate his duties to another person or entity; there may be another clause that restricts the artist's ability to assign the contract to another artist

Financial Clauses
These important clauses provide details outlining finances and recordkeeping:

- Commission Clause—outlines the commission schedule paid by artist to manager and usually includes a definition of *gross income*
- Gross Income Clause—provides a definition for what is commissionable; usually very broadly worded
- Recordkeeping Clause—provides artist with the right to receive periodic financial statements from manager
- Audit Clause—gives manager the right to inspect artist's financial records for some period after the contractual relationship ends if artist is still responsible to manager for continuing commission payments

Clauses Relating to Timing
As this grouping suggests, these clauses have something to do with timing:

- Term Clause—spells out the length of the contractual relationship
- Termination Clause—lays out the permissible way of cutting the contract term short
- Default/Notice Clause—says that if either party to the contract has an issue with the other's performance under the contract, he must give specific notice (*X* days) in a specific manner (usually in writing) and provide details

of the grievance; this clause often contains a notice period for the non-complaining party to change his behavior before the complaining party can allege that a breach has taken place

- Extension Clause—provides details for how and when the contract can be extended by some period
- Renewal Clause—provides for the circumstances under which the contract term will be automatically renewed

Housekeeping Clauses

Expect to see most or all of the following most commonly used contract clauses:

- Merger
- Amendment
- Severability
- Savings
- Choice of Law
- Forum
- Remedies
- Waiver
- Arbitration

There will likely be other clauses outlining how manager will be paid; whether manager can cash artist's engagement checks and pay himself commission; the expenses for which artist has sole responsibility; and other important arrangements.

AN ANNOTATED ARTIST-MANAGEMENT CONTRACT

What follows is an annotated artist-management agreement for a non-classical musician.

MANAGEMENT AGREEMENT

THIS AGREEMENT (the Agreement), made this ____day of May_____, 2018, the (Effective Date) is entered into by _____, hereinafter (Manager), and _____, hereinafter collectively known as (Artist), sometimes all parties referred to as Party or Parties.

RECITALS

WHEREAS Artist desires to perform as a group to be known as *X*; and

WHEREAS Artist desires to engage and appoint Manager to assist in Artist's career in the "entertainment industry" as a recording and performing artist to be known as *X*, in order to help maximize Artist's career; and

WHEREAS Manager desires to assist Artist develop Artist's career by handling the day to day business of the Artist to allow the Artist to create, write, record, tour, and otherwise fully and completely develop Artist's unique talent in the "entertainment industry."

> *These optional WHEREAS clause are called recitals. Although they are now considered old-fashioned, I like them because they provide some background for third-party readers to discern why the parties to a contract are entering into the agreement. The recitals provide context for all of the promises that follow.*

NOW, THEREFORE in consideration of the foregoing, and the mutual covenants[8] and agreements set forth herein, Artist and Manager hereby agree as follows:

> *The sentence immediate above is called the Mutuality Provision (offer and acceptance). It shows that the artist and manager are in agreement (have reached a meeting of the minds) and intend that their promises to each other will be contractually binding. Contracts aren't necessarily required to have the Mutuality Provision spelled out like this, but the idea that it embodies is absolutely required for a contract to be valid.*

1. Artist hereby engages and appoints Manager and Manager hereby accepts to be engaged as Artist's exclusive personal manager, representative and advisor, throughout the "territory" and during the "term," with respect to all of Artist's activities in the "entertainment industry," including but not limited to the following services:

a. Professional Management activities to:
   (1) supervise Artist's professional employment, and on Artist's behalf, to consult with employers and prospective employers so as to assure the proper use of and continued demand for Artist's services;
   (2) be available at reasonable times and places to confer with Artist in connection with all matters concerning Artist's professional career, business interests, employment and publicity;
   (3) with Artist's prior approval: engage, discharge and/or direct such theatrical agents, booking agencies and employment agencies, as well as other firms, persons or corporations that may be retained for the purpose of securing contracts, engagements or employment for Artist;
   (4) advise, counsel and guide Artist in the strategic management of Artist's career in the "entertainment industry";
   (5) assist Artist in meeting and forming relationships with key decision-makers in the "entertainment industry" relevant to Artist's talent and long-range career plans;
   (6) negotiate all contract terms, fees (including per diems where possible) on Artist's behalf and to fix the terms governing matters of disposition, use, employment or exploitation of Artist's talents and the products thereof;
   (7) represent Artist in all dealings with any union; and
   (8) accept payments on Artist's behalf and deposit and distribute such payments in accordance with protocols previously agreed upon by Artist and Manager as outlined in the revocable Power of Attorney;
b. Booking activities to assist Artist in obtaining employment showcasing Artist's talents in accordance with the strategic planning of Artist's career as agreed upon by and between Artist and Manager;
c. Administrative activities to:
   (1) prepare and package sample recordings and videos to submit to potential employers and booking agencies;
   (2) arrange auditions and meetings;
   (3) maintain all promotional supplies, organize, prepare, mail or otherwise transmit press kits and other promotional materials in support of Artist's appearances;

(4) provide general administrative support acting as a liaison with venue presenters; answering questions; solving problems and making decisions on Artist's behalf;

(5) make Artist's travel arrangements including accommodations; and

d. Publicity-related activities to:

(1) promote and publicize Artist's name and talent including organizing promotional interviews and photo sessions and setting up local radio and television spots;

(2) supervise, approve and permit any and all publicity, press notices, public relations and advertising;

(3) with Artist's prior approval: approve and permit the use of Artist's name, likeness, voice, sound effects, caricatures, literary, artistic and musical materials for the purpose of advertising, public relations, promotion and publicity for any and all of Artist's services and in promotion and advertising of any and all products or services;

(4) with Artist's prior approval: make arrangements with packagers, bookers, sponsors, theaters, radio, television, motion picture, etc. on Artist's behalf for Artist's services as well as agreements with talent or booking agencies. However, with respect to the services that are the subject of this Agreement, Artist reserves all rights and intends to retain administrative control of any and all social media accounts associated with Artist whether now in existence or to be created in the future; and

(5) with Artist's prior approval and at Artist's sole expense: engage a public relations firm to effectively present Artist's image before the public in a manner designed to further Artist's professional career.

Item 1 is the Scope of Engagement Clause. It lays out all of the services that the manager will provide to the artist. This clause must reflect all of the promises that the manager made to the artist, encompass the artist's expectations of what the manager will (and is realistically able to) do for the artist, and correspond with the content set out in the recitals. This clause should be very detailed for the benefit of the manager (for expectation setting), but also to keep the manager accountable to the artist. If this clause is vague, it will be very difficult, if not impossible, for the artist to criticize the manager's work and, if necessary, determine that he is in breach of his contractual duties.

This particular Scope of Engagement Clause is specific to the artist who signed with this manager. The artist's intentions are made clear via the items that the artist wishes to control (via artist's prior consent) and those things over which the artist wishes to exercise even greater control (requiring artist's prior written consent).

For managers who work in states that require talent agents to be licensed, as New York and California do, these Scope Clauses are often paired with a companion clause that says that the manager: (1) is not a licensed talent agent, and (2) is not responsible for procuring employment for the artist.

2. The territory of this Agreement (the "territory") shall be the United States of America, its territories and possessions, and Canada.

    This is the Territory Provision. It sets out the geographic territory for the manager's services. Managers will want the territory to be as broad as possible in order to be able to collect a commission for artists' work everywhere, but artists should limit the territory to only the territory where managers can reasonably expect to provide services. For example, some classical musicians have a U.S. manager and a European manager.

3. Artist's engagement and appointment of Manager shall be on an exclusive basis with Manager.

    This is an Exclusivity Clause. It means that the artist is agreeing that she will not engage another manager to work on her behalf. This is the clause that would be modified if the artist intended to engage a European manager in addition to her manager handling her engagements in the United States and Canada.

4. "Entertainment industry" means, without limitation, all services and activities, and the products thereof, in the fields of music, recording, concerts, public appearance, drama, literature, publishing, motion pictures, television, radio, television and radio commercials, including contracts for the packaging of the products of any of the foregoing for sale, license or other distribution, as well as any form of merchandising or other exploitation of Artist's services and activities (e.g., the use of any materials, trademarks, names, for clothing, toys, posters, games, endorsements and the like).

This contract is for a non-classical, non-theater musician. The definition of entertainment industry reflects this. It is important to note that whenever a word is defined in a contract, the drafter is attempting to narrow it in some way to something less than its colloquial meaning. For this reason, defined terms should be very carefully reviewed to be sure that nothing is being omitted. Defined terms are usually set out from all of the other words in a contract by bolding, italics, caps, quotation marks, or some combination of these indicators.

5. The term of this Agreement (the "term") shall commence on the Effective Date and continue for a period of two (2) years (Initial Period). Following expiration of the Initial Period, the "term" shall be automatically extended for successive, one (1) year periods, until "termination" by either party in accordance with this Agreement.

   This is the Term Clause. It sets out the initial length of the agreement (two years), but also says that the initial two-year term will automatically reinstate for additional one-year periods until terminated by either party in one of the permissible manners outlined within the contract.

6. As compensation for Manager's services hereunder, Artist agrees to pay to Manager (or Manager shall retain, if applicable) a sum equal to twenty percent (20%) of "gross compensation" (as defined hereinafter) derived from the products of Artist's services in the "territory" in connection with any and all engagements, contracts and agreements entered into, arranged or substantially negotiated prior to and during the "term" and extensions thereof (the "commission").

   This is the Commission Clause. It spells out what the manager's commission will be. Sometimes these clauses can be very elaborate, with different percentages payable for different types of artist engagements or for different sources of income. It is extremely important that some definition of income be used (this contract uses gross compensation) within this clause and that the definition that is used contemplates all sources of the artist's income that are subject to commission.

7. "Gross compensation" means the total of any and all forms of income, payments, consideration, compensation, or other things of value, including without limitation, salaries, actual fee advances, fees, royalties, bonuses, shares of receipts, stock and stock options, paid to Artist or applied for Artist's benefit directly or indirectly, reasonably related to Artist's activities in the "entertainment industry," less the following exclusions:

   a. sums pre-approved and paid by or on behalf of the Artist as budgeted, recoupable recording costs or budgeted recoupable video costs (i.e., other than actual advances or other payments to Artist that are subject to Manager's commission);

   b. royalties, actual advances or fees paid or credited by or on behalf of the Artist to any third party producers or mixers to a budget pre-approved by Artist;

   c. for the purposes of this Agreement Manager shall not charge commission on any compensation, as defined herein, received from the production, distribution and sale of the Artist's first album to be recorded in 2018; and

   d. living expense per diems, if any.

As noted above, this definition is very important. It is recommended that artists make a comprehensive list of all of their sources of past, current, and potential future income and make sure that the definition used in their management contract does not subject any sources of income to commission that they do not intend to pay commission on. For example, if you win a competition with a monetary prize, do you intend to pay 20% commission to your manager? If you accept a university position or other part-time salaried work, do you intend to pay commission on that? For how long?

Some of these issues can be points of contention. From the artist's perspective, she doesn't want to have to pay commission week after week on a part-time university salary for the rest of her teaching years. The manager's perspective would likely be that he designed, nurtured, and built the artist's career to the point that brought the artist to the level of prominence that attracted the university to her and, therefore, should be compensated the same way he otherwise would.

So, a balance must be reached for an equitable resolution of issues like this one. One solution is to just spell things like this out clearly and specifically in the contract. Another is to have issues involving any long-term arrangements subject to a Phase-Out Provision. A third option is to have a clause that, rather than subjecting long-term assignments like university jobs to commission, provides that to the extent that the manager negotiates a higher salary for such arrangements, the manager would be paid commission on only the difference he negotiated. For example, if the artist is offered a salary rate of $150 per teaching hour, but the manager negotiates a rate of $200 per teaching hour with the institution, the commission payable to the manager would be 20% of $50 per teaching hour, which would translate to $10 per teaching hour for the duration of the artist's tenure there.

These issues need to be fully considered by the artist, discussed with the manager, and clearly spelled out in the contract.

8. Manager's "commission" shall be paid in full for a period of two (2) years following expiration of the Initial Period and any extensions thereof; following such two year period, Manager's commission shall be payable at a fifty (50%) percent reduced rate for one (1) year, then payable at a seventy-five (75%) percent reduced rate for one (1) year, then payable at a eighty-seven and one half (87.5%) percent reduced rate for one (1) year, after which no further "commission" payments shall be due ("post-term commission").

This is the Post-Term Commission Clause (also known as a Phase-Out Clause). It's a version of a Sunset Clause, but in addition to putting an end date to something that continues after the contract's end, as a Sunset Clause does, it also phases something out, slowly, over time. In this case, it walks the commission amount due to the manager down over a period of years. The reason for clauses like this one is an effort to find a mutually agreeable solution that balances out the realities of properly compensating the manager for work or deals the manager procured for the artist during the term of the contract and putting some reasonable cap on the amount of commission the artist has to pay the manager long after the artist-manager relationship has ended. These are often a point of contention, but should nonetheless be worked out thoroughly early in the negotiation process—

especially for artists who expect or intend to make recordings or enter into long-term commitments, like long-running Broadway shows or university teaching assignments.

9. Artist shall be solely responsible for payment of Artist's own expenses (e.g., equipment, travel, accounting, legal and living expenses), booking agencies' fees, union dues, publicity costs, promotional or exploitation costs and reasonable expenses arising from the performance by Manager of services hereunder, and Manager shall have no liability for same. Manager shall not be required to travel; however, when Manager does travel it shall be at Artist's expense and upon prior consultation with, and approval by, Artist, provided Artist is reasonably available for such consultation. Unless otherwise agreed on a case-by-case basis, Artist agrees to promptly reimburse Manager for all expenses which Manager advances or incurs on Artist's behalf (e.g., travel, lodging and related expenses).

It's always a good idea to work out, in advance, the amount and nature of reimbursable expenses that the manager can incur on the artist's behalf without the artist's prior consent. Nobody likes to be surprised with an end-of-month e-mail saying that they have to reimburse someone. Additionally, artists will not want to fund a startup manager's business-building costs. Best practice would be to identify and determine the amounts of the most common types of expenses likely to be incurred by the manager and write them into the contract. Then, put some type of dollar cap on any other, non-identified expenses that could come up.

10. Manager may audit Artist's books and records pertaining to the payment of the commission and "post-term commission" to Manager hereunder once during a particular calendar year and only once with respect to each accounting and only within three (3) years after the date each such accounting is rendered to Manager. Any action or proceeding related to accountings hereunder must be commenced, if at all, within four (4) years after the date of the statement concerned.

This is an Audit Provision. This one is a bit unusual in that it gives the audit right to the manager (this artist is apparently taking on some sales responsibilities and then remitting commission to the manager. The manager wants to be sure he is being paid commission on 100% of the artist's income). The "post-term commission" part of this clause is standard. It allows the manager to audit the artist's financial records relating to this contract for three years following the termination of their contractual relationship. The final sentence of this clause is creating a four-year contractual statute of limitations on the manager's ability to bring any claims or actions (such as a lawsuit or an independent third-party accounting) against the artist for failure to pay the right commission amount. This four-year period may be more or less than what the law provides in the jurisdiction governing the contract.

11. Manager shall maintain complete and accurate books and records relating to this Agreement, including, but not limited to: (1) an accounting of all Artist's "gross compensation" as defined herein and received by Manager; (2) all "commissions" due to Manager; and (3) all receipts for any and all reimbursable expenses incurred by Manager relating to this Agreement. Manager shall make books and records available to Artist not less frequently than monthly.

    This is the Recordkeeping Provision. It allows the artist to review the manager's financial records (only as they relate to the artist) at least monthly. Even if you never intend to monitor your manager's records, you will want to have the right to do so at least quarterly, if not monthly.

12. Artist acknowledges that Manager is an independent contractor, not exclusive to Artist, and may perform the same or similar services for others as are contemplated hereunder. It being specifically understood that Manager is acting hereunder as an independent contractor, this Agreement is not intended to create, and nothing contained herein shall be construed to create, a partnership between Artist and Manager.

    This clause is common to artist-management contracts. It does a few things: (1) it says that manager is not exclusive to the artist (manager has other clients too), and (2) it establishes that the relationship between the artist and the manager is not a partnership. This part is included because sometimes a partnership is found by courts where none was intended. Partners in partnerships owe special duties to one another, such as sharing profits and business liabilities. Also, partners owe a heightened duty of loyalty to each other, and this is something that a manager can't always provide to all of his artists simultaneously.

13. Artist and Manager acknowledge that this Agreement relates to management services to be rendered to the Artist in their performances and productions under the group name of X, or such other name Artist collectively may perform under. And, the Artist may have separate management with regard to them performing individually and not as X.

This clause acknowledges that members of this group/band sometimes perform as individuals and that income from that work is not subject to commission under this contract.

14. The parties shall be entitled to Terminate this Agreement, following expiration of the Initial Period, upon ninety (90) days prior written notice to the other party ("termination"). Manager shall have sixty (60) days following "termination" to fulfill and/or finalize any commitments, obligations and/or duties commenced during the "term" pursuant to this Agreement. "Termination" shall in no way affect the commission, "post-term commission" and any reimbursements due to Manager under this Agreement.

This is a Termination Clause. All longer-term contracts should have one. The clause should spell out that the manager has continuing responsibilities to tie up any outstanding items and support any gigs for which he will be collecting a commission after the contract term has ended. Similarly, it tells the artist that even though the contract has ended, the artist is still responsible for paying commission on work procured by the manager during the contract period and still must reimburse the manager for any outstanding expenses. This example requires either party to give ninety days' notice of intent to not renew the contract.

15. Artist warrants and represents that:
    a. Artist is under no legal disability and has the right to enter into this Agreement and perform its terms; and

b. no act or omission by Artist will violate the rights of any person, firm or corporation or will subject Manager to any liability or claims.

This is a Representation and Warranty Clause. These can be written in many ways, and the content will depend on what the other party wants the artist to affirmatively state. This one requires the artist to state: (1) that the artist is who he says he is, without misrepresentation (which can be a basis for rescinding a contract); (2) that the artist is mentally and legally competent to contract; and (3) that the artist is not under any obligation to another manager (or other) that could potentially subject this manager to legal liability for entering into this contract with the artist. Item 17, below, holds the artist legally accountable to the manager for any lawsuits that might come up as the result of these promises.

16. Limited Power of Attorney. Artist agrees to execute a short form revocable power of attorney, which Manager shall be entitled to file in any jurisdiction.

This clause references a Power of Attorney Clause but doesn't actually attempt to build one into the contract itself. Such clauses are of questionable validity since most, if not all, states require a separate, notarized document that contains state-specific language. Not everyone is comfortable signing a power of attorney, and if you're one of those people, don't do it. I wouldn't unless there was a very good reason and the power provided a very specific right to achieve only that goal. But, if you don't sign one, expect to remain available and respond quickly if your manager needs your signature on a contract. Today, with electronic signatures and the ability to scan and e-mail documents, it's less of an issue than it was in the past.

If you are comfortable giving your manager power of attorney, be sure that it is very narrowly drawn (no broader than it needs to be to expedite the manager's work for you). Artists are most frequently asked to provide powers for managers to sign their names to contracts (thereby binding the artists to those contracts) and to sign artists' checks. In any case, do not sign an irrevocable power of attorney; you want to be able to retract the power(s) given at any time.

17. Artist agrees to indemnify and hold Manager harmless against any damages, liability, costs, expenses and fees (including reasonable attorney's fees) incurred as a result of or in connection with any claim or proceeding against Manager arising out of any breach or alleged breach of any warranty, representation or covenant made by Artist in this Agreement. Manager agrees to indemnify and hold Artist harmless against any damages, liability, costs, expenses and fees (including reasonable attorney's fees) arising out of Manager's actual or alleged wrongful acts committed or alleged to have been committed in connection with this Agreement.

This is an Indemnification Clause. It is largely bilateral, meaning that each party is making the same promises to the other with respect to indemnification. Indemnification clauses usually contain two promises: (1) the promise to hire legal counsel to defend the other party against legal claims made against that party for something you have done or are alleged to have done relating to the agreement; and (2) the promise to pay any monetary amount (damages) awarded against that party and you for those same claims. This clause also makes the artist responsible for providing a defense and indemnifying the manager for any claims relating to the representations and warranties (from item 15, above) made by the artist to the manager.

18. As a condition precedent to any assertion by either party that the other is in default or in breach of an obligation hereunder, the claiming party must advise the other in writing of the specific facts upon which the claim is based and of the specific nature of the breach or default and the other party shall have a period of thirty (30) days after receipt of such notice to cure such breach or default. During that period, no breach shall be deemed incurable.

This clause is called a Default (or Notice of Cure) Provision. It's a good clause to have because it requires that if either party to the contract has an issue with the other party's actions or inactions, each must provide written notice to the other of that issue and give them adequate time to address the issue or deficiency (thirty days in this case) before the party with the complaint can assert that the other party is in breach of their contractual obligations. This clause helps to keep the agreement on track and maintain the business relationship.

19. All notices or reports permitted or required under this Agreement shall be in writing and shall be delivered by personal delivery, electronic mail (e-mail), facsimile transmission or by certified or registered mail, return receipt requested, and shall be deemed given upon personal delivery, five (5) days after deposit in the mail, or upon acknowledgment of receipt or other proof of electronic transmission. Notices shall be sent to the addresses set forth at the end of this Agreement or such other address as either Party may specify in writing.

    This is a Notices Clause. It merely lays out how the parties should communicate important notices to one another such as Default or Termination notices.

20. Any provisions of this Agreement which by their nature should survive "termination" or expiration or remain to be performed after "termination" or expiration, shall remain in full force and effect.

    This clause underscores this manager's interest in making sure that the artist understands that the contract contains some clauses laying out responsibilities that will outlast the term of the contract itself and that those clauses are intended to be fully enforceable.

21. This Agreement may only be assigned by Manager to an entity in which Manager has a controlling interest provided, however, that Manager shall remain responsible to Artist for the services contracted hereunder and see that each is competently performed.

    This is a unilateral Assignment Clause. It allows the manager to subcontract his duties under this contract (all of the services indicated in the Scope of Engagement Clause, item 1), but requires that if the manager exercises this right, he is still responsible to the artist to see that each of those enumerated duties is competently carried out. Further, it restricts the manager's assigning to only those organizations in which the manager has a majority ownership interest. If it did not have this limitation, the manager could just pass off all of his duties to another agency or person. If you, as the artist, want a specific manager to handle your career and no one else, then ask for a Key Man Clause to be added to your contract.

22. Artist may not assign this Agreement or any of Artist's rights hereunder, without prior approval of Manager.

    This is a more standard use of an Assignment Clause. It restricts the artist from assigning her duties to another musician. This type of clause is very common in personal services contracts even though they only restate what the law already provides.

23. This Agreement is binding upon and shall inure to the benefit of the parties' respective heirs, executors, administrators, successors and assignees. If any provision hereof is determined invalid or unenforceable by a court of competent jurisdiction, the portion determined to be invalid or unenforceable shall not affect the validity and enforceability of the remaining provisions hereof.

    This bundled clause does two things: (1) it provides that in the event that one of the parties dies, becomes incompetent, declares bankruptcy, or has assigned her rights or duties to a third party, that third party is entitled to benefit from any income due (or liabilities owing) under this contract as though it was the original party to the contract; and (2) the second sentence is a Severability Clause that says that if any portion of the contract is not in harmony with the law, it will be carved out of the contract and the remaining portions will remain, minus the offending portion.

24. This Agreement shall be governed by the laws of the state of Pennsylvania. Any controversy or claim arising out of or relating to any provision of this Agreement, or the breach thereof, shall be submitted to arbitration in accordance with the commercial rules then obtained, of the American Arbitration Association. The arbitrator's powers shall be limited to the interpretation of the terms of this Agreement and the arbitrator shall have no power to vary these terms. The judgment rendered in such proceeding

shall be conclusive and binding upon the parties hereto and may be entered in any court of competent jurisdiction.

This is a bundled Choice of Law (or Governing Law) Clause and an Arbitration Clause (which, in reality, acts as a Forum [or Venue] Clause). Pennsylvania has been chosen as the state whose law will provide the backdrop of this agreement. If any disputes arise between the artist and the manager, they have agreed, in advance, to submit those issues to an arbitrator (rather than file a lawsuit) and have the dispute handled in Pennsylvania.

25. This Agreement represents the entire understanding of the parties with respect to the subject matter hereof and may be modified or amended only by a writing signed by both parties. No waiver of any breach of this Agreement shall be construed as a continuing waiver or consent to any subsequent breach hereof.

This is another bundled clause. It contains a Merger Clause, an Amendment Clause, and a Waiver Clause.

Merger Clause: The first part of the first sentence states that this contract contains the entire understanding of the parties and that there are no side deals. These are important clauses because they trigger a rule of evidence that precludes a judge or other intermediary from hearing any evidence, written or oral, that contradicts any of the terms in the contract. This clause underscores the importance of being sure that every detail that was negotiated and agreed to is clearly provided for in the contract, because if this clause is in your contract, you will not be able to provide any proof to support missing information or promises.

Amendment Clause: The second part of the first sentence contains the Amendment Clause. This clause makes good sense because it restricts any party's ability to make unilateral changes to the contract.

Waiver Clause: The second sentence contains a Waiver Clause, which says that should one of the parties choose not to take issue with, or otherwise allow, one of the enumerated restrictions or requirements in the contract,

then that party is not completely waiving that same restriction or require-
ment in the future. The analogy I use is a teenager asking his parents to
extend his curfew for some special occasion. Just because the parents grant
this exception one time doesn't mean they have changed the original curfew
time—they've only waived it for this special occasion. Waiver Clauses oper-
ate the same way.

26. This Agreement may be executed in counterparts and transmitted by
    facsimile copy, each of which shall constitute an original and which taken
    together shall constitute the Agreement.

    This clause merely points out that all parties to the contract need not sign
    the original contract in order for it to be valid.

IN WITNESS WHEREOF, Artist and Manager hereto have executed this
Agreement on the day and year first written above.

_____   _____
By: (*Artist*)   Date   By: (*Manager*)   Date

Address _____   Address _____

Part IV

RESOURCES

9

Self-Help

Let's face it: sometimes things go wrong. Try not to assign blame; that's useless. When we assign blame, we cloud our judgment and this undermines our ability to find a timely and adequate solution. Often, when a problem arises, it's an honest mistake, a blunder. In my twenty-plus years working in business, it was very rare that someone was genuinely out to sabotage or undermine another.

Don't get me wrong: businesspeople can and do look for opportunities to advance their own agendas, but it's usually obvious when this happens. They're very upfront about it because their agenda is their central purpose for the relationship—usually to make money for themselves and/or the entity they represent. Businesspeople understand this and are less likely to take these issues personally than those who are new to practicing in a business environment. And it is practicing; the more you do it, the easier it becomes. Consider working with contracts to be another skill you can develop for the advancement of your career.

The best way to avoid contract disputes is to understand what you want, clearly ask for it upfront, and then check to see whether it was given to you in the contract before you sign it.

Once you learn the appropriate way to express yourself when you need to exercise your rights, doing so won't feel like a death match. Besides, you're more than halfway there already—you've been studying up on what your rights are and preparing for this possibility, right?

NEGOTIATION, NOT LITIGATION

Restating what was discussed in the introduction, most business disputes are resolved by compromise provided both parties are open to it. In contract disputes, this means renegotiating one or more of the original terms to the satisfaction of both parties.

Choosing negotiation over litigation (or threats of litigation) serves several important purposes:

1. It shows you to be a businessperson possessing business skills, and this gives you something in common with the other party to the dispute (usually a presenter, agent, or manager).
2. It shows you to be reasonable and puts the other party more at ease.
3. It shows a good faith willingness to attempt to resolve the matter outside the legal system—something judges look for and appreciate when they see it.
4. It preserves your reputation and goodwill—you never want a reputation for being difficult or rigid.
5. Most important, it preserves the business relationship *even if* you decide you don't like the other party's business practices and don't intend to work with them again.

HYPOTHETICAL SCENARIO #1: YOUR CONTRACTED GIG IS CANCELED

You are hired to musically prepare and conduct a production of Wagner's *Tristan und Isolde* for the Nebraska Wagner Society. You have a signed contract, but two months before your scheduled arrival date, you receive a call/letter/e-mail stating that the production will not take place (an *anticipatory breach of contract* like the one I reference in the preface).

You need to know what the presenter, the Nebraska Wagner Society, plans to do about it. You know that you are entitled to your fee and that you are required to *mitigate* your *damages* (accept similar work, if possible, during that time period and deduct the expenses you would have incurred had the other party not canceled).

Self-Help

You know your rights. Try to pursue them on your own before seeking legal help. Typically, you have several years to bring a *breach of contract* action against the other party if you need to. Litigation remains in the background as an option if the following self-help efforts fail.

1. **Identify the statute of limitations.** Many artists' contracts are constructed under a New York Choice of Law Clause where the statute of limitations (SOL) is six years for a breach of contract claim. Other states many have shorter SOLs, so look up the SOL in the state whose law governs your deal and see how much time you have. Once the statute runs out, you are usually out of luck.

   You never want to even get close to the statutory limit. The longer you wait, the harder it will be to get the outcome you are entitled to. Knowing your rights and knowing you are ready to exercise them is what gives you the basis to assert them without litigation. If the other side knows you're serious and that you might win, compromise is possible.

   In *Contracts: The Essential Business Desk Reference*, Richard Stim provides a handy chart for state statutes of limitations. Nolo's website also provides a chart at http://www.nolo.com/legal-encyclopedia/statute-of-limitations-state-laws-chart-29941.html.

2. **Call first; don't write.** When a contract problem arises, call the other party and see what you can work out amicably. If you immediately write to them—particularly if you send letters via registered mail with return receipts, you put them on the defensive because they will see that you are keeping records to potentially use against them. Save this tactic for later.

3. **Script it.** Don't be above writing a script for this call (see Example 9.1). Lawyers do this all the time. In fact, one lawyer friend of mine joked that she wouldn't order in lunch without a script! The tone of your phone call can be friendly and casual, but you also must be firm—this is a business conversation that concerns your livelihood. Do not apologize for knowing or exercising your rights.

EXAMPLE 9.1

PHONE CALL SCRIPT

You: Hello, Mr. Slithering. This is Oprah Singer. I received your letter regarding the cancellation of the Nebraska Wagner Society's production of *Tristan und Isolde*. I am sorry to hear about the fiscal problems weighing upon NWS. This cancellation is a loss to the entire community—not only those associated with this production. I have every expectation that an organization such as the NWS will quickly rebound from this unfortunate setback. I'm calling to inquire about my fee. When can I expect to receive it?

He: Ms. Singer, I wish I could help you out, but it is not our position to pay people for not working!

You: Mr. Slithering, as you know, I set time aside in my schedule for this production and, unfortunately, I was unable to replace this period with other work. I'm not asking for a gift. We have a contract and NWS breached that contract. I'm only asking for what the law requires under such circumstances.

He: Well, you know, we simply don't have the funds or else we wouldn't have canceled the production. And if people like you press us to pay for work they don't do, it will force us to close our doors. Do you want that?

(Don't fall for this nonsense. If the company were run in a fiscally more prudent way, it wouldn't be in this situation.)

You: Please take this matter to your board and get back to me within the next thirty days. Thank you.

4. **Keep records.** Keep a detailed record of everything that was said as soon as the conversation is over—especially anything promised to you and any time frames associated with those promises.
5. **Reinforce.** Then, send a business-style e-mail outlining what was discussed or agreed to during the phone call.

6. **Send a letter.** It's up to you how much you want to follow up with additional calls and e-mails, but after a few weeks without a response, it's clearly time to send a letter. Send it via registered mail and pay for a return receipt. The receipt will:

- provide proof that your letter was sent and received;
- help with your recordkeeping;
- tell you who, specifically, signed for your letter; and
- send the message that you are focused, organized, serious, and ready to pursue the matter. And if you ever do need to hire an attorney, your records will come in handy for the attorney and be necessary for the court or for an arbitrator to see your good faith efforts to resolve the issue yourself—especially if you offer a reasonable compromise that is rejected.

In the hypothetical given, you are legally entitled to 100% of the engagement fee you contracted for minus expenses, but be open to compromise. Offering one will go a long way with the presenter and with a judge if it gets to that. Compromise is very common in the arts. Don't think of it as being weak—it's good business practice and will go far toward preserving the business relationship and, more important, your reputation in a relatively small business community.

The Business Letter
Writing a business letter/e-mail is where many creative people go wrong. It's not their fault—few have ever been taught how to write a business letter. It's surprisingly easy. These letters may seem short and stark if you're not used to them, but there's no need for creativity.

Here are the essentials:

1. Keep the letter short and simple.
2. Include only the facts—save the emotion for your performances.
3. Be firm but polite.
4. Be reasonable. This means understanding how non-profit organizations operate. Smaller organizations may have a dual check-signing requirement (imposed on them by their board or even by their insurance company). They may also need to call a meeting to make certain decisions and obtain

approval, by vote count, to write checks over a certain amount or for purposes other than standard payments.

What *not* to do in a business letter:

1. Do not use emotion phrases like "I think," "I feel," "This is unfair."
2. Do not make threats of any kind.
3. Do not engage in name-calling.

Send your non-electronic letters via registered mail (U.S. Postal Service) with return receipts. You can use a different delivery service if you prefer, but be sure that someone at the other end signs and acknowledges receipt of your letters *and that you have a record of it*. As mentioned above, this will also serve to put the presenter on notice that you are keeping records.

Burn No Bridges

People who work in this space tend to change jobs frequently. If you think you can burn this one bridge, you're wrong. You would be burning several—one with each person who works there *and* then at any organization those people move to throughout their careers. So, be careful: express yourself professionally even through anger and frustration.

And *please* don't take your campaign to social media! You've worked too hard and sacrificed too much to flush it all away in a moment of frustration.

SAMPLE BUSINESS LETTERS

This section provides three samples asking for relief (money).

- Letter #1: Example 9.2 is a follow-up e-mail you could use after calling the presenter. You are writing to confirm the details of your conversation or, if you were unable to speak to the presenter, to document the voicemail you left.
- Letter #2: Example 9.3, is the first follow-up letter. It references your first attempts at reaching the presenter by phone and e-mail.
- Letter #3: Example 9.4, is the second follow-up/final letter referencing past calls and letters.

Note the dates on the letters/e-mails. The dates reflect the reality that some, especially smaller, non-profit organizations need time to respond to any type of request, but especially requests that are outside their normal everyday business practices (like writing engagement fee checks for performances that never took place).

If your self-help efforts fail, you need to decide whether to pursue the matter through legal means—a lawsuit. If you choose this route, you can look for free legal assistance through a free or low-cost legal clinic (or an attorney referral service) that is associated with a state or local (county or city) bar association. If you decide to speak with an attorney, print out all your supporting records (including your contract), organize your paperwork chronologically, and bring all of it with you to that meeting.

See Resources, later in this chapter, for help locating an attorney in your area.

EXAMPLE 9.2

PHONE CALL FOLLOW-UP E-MAIL LETTER

January 1, 2018

One Beantown Way
Boston, MA 02111
day (617) 333-3333
cell (617) 333-3331

Nigel Slithering, President
Nebraska Wagner Society
121 Flat Way
Omaha, NE 34443
Re: Canceled *Tristan* Production

Dear Mr. Slithering,

As we discussed, my contract calls for me to be paid $_____. Despite NWS's difficulties, I'll need to be paid the full amount of my engagement fee under the contract by _____.

I requested that this matter be presented to the NWS Board for consideration and asked for a response from you by February 1, 2018.

Thank you,

Oprah Singer

EXAMPLE 9.3

FIRST FOLLOW-UP LETTER

February 1, 2018

One Beantown Way
Boston, MA 02111
day (617) 333-3333
cell (617) 333-3331

Nigel Slithering, President
Nebraska Wagner Society
121 Flat Way
Omaha, NE 34443
Re: Canceled *Tristan* Production

Dear Mr. Slithering,

I have not heard from you regarding my call(s) of _____ or my e-mail of January 1, 2018, to confirm that payment of my engagement fee for the canceled production of *Tristan und Isolde* is forthcoming.

Kindly confirm that it is and the date which I can expect to receive it.

Thank you,

Oprah Singer

EXAMPLE 9.4

SECOND FOLLOW-UP/FINAL LETTER

February 15, 2018

One Beantown Way
Boston, MA 02111
day (617) 333-3333
cell (617) 333-3331

Nigel Slithering, President
Nebraska Wagner Society
121 Flat Way
Omaha, NE 34443
Re: Canceled *Tristan* Production

Dear Mr. Slithering,

I have not heard from you regarding my call(s) of _____ or my e-mails/letters of January 1 and February 1, 2018. Please forward my full fee of $_____ for the 2018 canceled production of *Tristan und Isolde* within 15 days of receipt of this letter.

If I don't hear from you by March 1, I will turn this matter over to _____, my attorney, who can be reached at _____.

Thank you,

Oprah Singer

HYPOTHETICAL SCENARIO #2: SAME AS ABOVE, BUT YOU HAVE NO WRITTEN CONTRACT TO PERFORM

In this hypothetical, you believe you have a *valid, enforceable oral contract*. To clarify this belief, you need to walk through the *validity* and *enforceability* analyses discussed in Chapter 2.

Remember, if the gig was more than a year away from the date likely entered into the oral contract, you have nothing to enforce because it doesn't meet the requirements of the Statute of Frauds in the jurisdiction governing your situation.

If you think you have an oral contract, then start to gather all the supporting documentation that outlines the arrangement: e-mails, notes, transcribed voicemail messages, etc., and follow the self-help process outlined above, but reference your belief that an *oral* contract exists between you and the presenter in your communications. See chapter 2 for an explanation of Statute of Frauds.

HYPOTHETICAL SCENARIO #3: YOU HAVE CONTRACTED TO PERFORM, BUT NOW WOULD LIKE TO SUBSTITUTE SOMEONE ELSE

There are any number of reasons why you might want to get out of a gig after you've committed yourself to doing it, but realize that you cannot just find a substitute for yourself. Because musicians' contracts to perform are *personal services contracts*, special rules apply.

Recall from Chapter 7 that the general rule for assigning one's duties under a *general services contract* is that you may do it provided that your contract doesn't restrict it (via an Assignment Clause). If you do subcontract those duties to another person, you remain responsible to the other party to the contract for ensuring that those duties are competently performed.

However, because you signed a *personal services contract* for your unique services, you may not subcontract the duty to perform to another person, however competent he or she may be, unless your contract specifically allows it. This rule is true even if your contract doesn't specifically disallow it.

So, what you should do is call the other party to your contract, tell them your situation, and ask whether they can release you from the contract. Have a short list of other musicians you have already contacted whose competence you can vouch for, who are available to perform the engagement date(s) and any rehearsal(s) you had agreed to, and who are willing to do the engagement for the rate you accepted. If a substitute musician requires more money than you agreed to, you should make up that difference.

The other party to your contract might prefer to find its own substitute for you, but your legwork and offer to help will show some professionalism and, hopefully, not jeopardize the relationship for future work with this person or organization.

SPEAK WITH AN ATTORNEY WHEN . . .

1. **You are served with legal papers (service of suit).** If you are served with legal papers for any reason, contact an attorney. Ignoring the situation won't make it go away. If you miss a court date and don't respond to a summons, you can have a default judgment rendered against you. This means you've lost the dispute without ever having an opportunity to tell your side of the story.

2. **You incurred expenses in anticipation of a job, believing that a contract was forthcoming.** Scenario: You were told by a presenter that they were desperate to find a replacement for an ailing musician. You are one of only a handful of people who are familiar with the score and could replace him. You believe that contract details are being worked out, and you purchase airfare to get you to the venue only to be told later that day that they've engaged someone else. Under this scenario, you don't have a contract, so claiming that a *breach* or an *anticipatory breach* took place is likely not a possibility. However, by purchasing the airfare you changed your position to your detriment when you relied on what the presenter said to you. So, if the presenter refuses to reimburse you, you may be able to recover the airfare expenses under the theory of reliance. Situations like this are more complicated, but not insurmountable. Speak to an attorney about this type of scenario.

3. **You are offered a recording contract.** This book provides guidance for understanding the many clauses and other specialized language contained in your contracts, but recording contracts are especially complicated—particularly with respect to the topics of royalty accounting—so it is highly advisable that you contact a person with specialized knowledge and actual experience in negotiating recording contracts. Further, even if your manager is an attorney, I recommend that you hire an independent, impartial person who can handle the negotiations and analyze your recording contract as an arm's-length transaction. Meaning, one who has no potential for a conflict of interest because she has no financial benefit from the contract.

RESOURCES: LEGAL

Do you need an attorney? This is something only you can decide based on your confidence about handling the issue yourself. Certainly, if you are having difficulty getting paid for work you've done, you should write a business letter laying out the facts and politely but firmly ask when you can expect payment. Send your letter by certified mail with a return receipt request, which requires someone's signature.

If you have a contract dispute and have decided to engage an attorney for help, you likely don't need an entertainment lawyer unless the issue is particularly complicated. For example, if the issue involves computations of royalties, copyright, or the signing of a record deal, you should engage an entertainment lawyer. Otherwise, you just need an attorney who has some understanding of what you do and what is standard in your industry.

Look for an attorney who is a member of her state bar association's Entertainment Law section and inquire whether the attorney usually handles artist matters or agent/manager matters. You will likely want an attorney who successfully handles issues facing artists. Regardless, if the attorney represents your specific manager in other matters, she will have a conflict and attorney ethical rules preclude her from taking you as a client.

Free or Low-Cost Legal Advice

State and local bar associations often have free or low-cost legal clinics where you can speak with an attorney directly. Sometimes these are walk-in clinics and sometimes you need to make an appointment in advance. If you go to one of these clinics with any kind of contract issue (including apartment lease disputes), make sure you bring the contract with you. Lawyers cannot give you legal advice if they don't know what the contract says. Note that these clinics provide advice, not representation, but many also operate as a referral service if you need a lawyer who specializes in a certain area.

You've likely heard of Volunteer Lawyers for the Arts (VLA, www.vlany .org). VLA is a national organization that exists to assist non-profit groups with their legal needs. Typically, this organization provides an opportunity for lawyers with an interest in the arts to perform pro bono (free) work and their law firm gets credit for the work. Individual VLA organizations may or may not be willing to help you, as an individual, with legal advice, but give them a try to be sure. If you work for a non-profit arts organization and need legal advice, do contact them for help.

Bar Associations
The American Bar Association (ABA) provides an online listing of state and local bar associations:

http://shop.americanbar.org/ebus/ABAGroups/DivisionforBarServices/Bar AssociationDirectories/StateLocalBarAssociations.aspx. You can use this site to see whether any associations near you offer free/low-cost legal clinics or attorney referral services.

For example, these three groups offer services in New York City:

- New York City Bar Association (Monday Night Clinic)
www.nycbar.org
(212) 626-7373
- New York Legal Assistance Group
www.nylag.org
(212) 613-5000
- LGBT Bar Association of Greater New York (Tuesday Night Clinic)
www.le-gal.org
(212) 620-7310

In addition to bar association clinics, some law schools also operate legal clinics where law students gain valuable experience providing counsel to clients under the guidance of lawyer-professors. Check the ABA website for accredited law schools in your area and then go to the schools' websites to see whether they operate legal clinics.

Some Helpful Law Websites
www.nololaw.com
www.cornell.edu
www.findlaw.com
www.kentlaw.com
http://jec.unm.edu
www.starvingartistslaw.org

RESOURCES: BOOKS

Below is a list of books available now that provide extensive details on various topics relating to the business of being a professional musician.

Being a Professional Musician

These four books are the most comprehensive I have seen in this genre, and all are excellent. Anyone serious about working in the music industry should own at least one of them. They focus on much of the same material, but take different approaches and use different styles.

1. *Beyond Talent: Creating a Successful Career in Music* by Angela Myles Beeching (Oxford University Press)

   As the title suggests, this book emphasizes the reality that to be successful in today's ultra-competitive music scene requires more than just talent—it requires some creativity, savvy business skills, and a lot of self-knowledge. This practical guide is a very easy read, making it perfect for those who are completely baffled about how to launch a career as a professional musician. There are chapters on networking, social media marketing, artist management, creative programming, funding for special projects, and much more. I would put this book in the "must" category for emerging artists of all genres, including non-musicians, because the content is readily transferrable to anyone interested in forging a career in the creative arts.

2. *The Musician's Business and Legal Guide*, edited by Mark Halloran (Pearson Prentice Hall)

   My favorite of these next three is Halloran's book. Its tone is conversational; he uses plenty of repetition within each chapter to help with comprehension, particularly when complicated concepts or legal terms are used; and he calls upon different industry experts for each topic or subtopic, which lends credibility to the content. I also like that different contract types are included, such as samples of a recording contract, a producer agreement, a personal manager contract, and a songwriter's co-publishing agreement. These are analyzed for attorneys, not musicians or other lay readers.

3. *This Business of Music: The Definitive Guide to the Music Industry* by M. William Krasilovsky and Sydney Shemel (Watson-Guptill)

   This excellent book, intended for musicians in the popular music genre, contains a lot of technical information for those interested in learning about the recording industry generally (distribution and labor agreements, music publishing and licensing, songwriter contracts and royalties, and music piracy and technology). It contains a CD-ROM of sample contracts, but it doesn't explain the clauses within those contracts or tell readers how to identify them. This book is very popular for good reason, but may be too technical for most lay readers. I can see it being especially useful for attorneys new to entertainment work.

4. *All You Need to Know about the Music Business* by Donald S. Passman (Simon and Schuster)

   Though Passman's book has a short section on the distinction between popular music and classical music recording contracts, it is clearly written for non-classical musicians. This conversational and often funny book offers the best advice I've seen for musicians interested in learning about the music business. He breaks down the lingo and talks about how to choose a business team and what each person's role should be in the artist's professional life. The book's most distinguishing features are: (a) real-life formulas and computations relating to record deals (royalties, advances, recoupments, and cross-collateralization); and (b) the outstanding advice Passman provides to songwriters for setting up their own publishing companies.

Contract Law

1. *Contract Law for Dummies* by Scott Burnham (John Wiley and Sons)

   Chock full of detail, *Contract Law for Dummies* is organized like all the other Dummies guides. It's very easy to maneuver through, has icons that alert readers to things to be cautious about, provides reminders of important details, cites key cases that have defined a given concept, and provides plenty of examples. While an excellent book for lawyers and law students, it may provide too much, and too in-depth, content for the casual reader.

2. *Contracts: The Essential Business Desk Reference* by Richard Stim (Nolo)

I love this book. It's set up like a dictionary of contract terms, arranged in alphabetical order with plenty of cross-referencing throughout. It's extremely easy to use and frequently provides examples. For readers looking for a comprehensive desk reference for contract terms, this would be the first book I'd buy. It also contains a handy chart for state statutes of limitation for breach of contract actions (both for written and for oral contracts).

Law Dictionaries
Black's Law Dictionary by Henry Campbell Black (West Publishing)

Akin to a *Webster's English Dictionary*, this impressive, formal dictionary is a must for lawyers (and law students) and a nice-to-have for everyone else. For those who prefer something less comprehensive, look for *Gilbert's Law Dictionary* instead. *Gilbert's* can be found in paperback. It's much smaller, cheaper, and less daunting than *Black's*.

Musician Contract Form Books
There are also contract form books compiled by publishers Hal Leonard (*Music Business Contract Library*) and by Berklee Press (*Music Industry Forms*). I haven't seen either of these compilations, but it sounds as though they are a collection of contract forms contained on CDs. I don't know if the forms are annotated or whether any explanations are provided for their use.

Intellectual Property Rights
Patent, Copyright & Trademark by Stephen Elias and edited by
Lisa Goldoftas (Nolo)

This book will be most helpful to composers, songwriters, performance artists, and others who create things and put them into tangible form. It provides an excellent primer for those new to these concepts, explains what legal protections are available, and advises how best to use them based on your needs. For example, the Copyright section has sample forms and fee information for registering a work with the U.S. Copyright Office. Further, it explains the difference between common law protection and the broader protection available to you (at low cost) if you register your creation.

Social Media Marketing

Social Media Marketing Workbook by Jason McDonald (JM Internet Group)

This book provides readers with step-by-step mini-guides on how to market their services (or goods) using Facebook, Twitter, YouTube, LinkedIn Marketing, Pinterest, and Yelp Local.

Notes

CHAPTER 1

1. Child Welfare Information Gateway, *Mandatory Reporters of Child Abuse and Neglect* (Washington, DC: US Department of Health and Human Services, Children's Bureau, 2014).

CHAPTER 2

1. A restrictive covenant is a promise to forego a right that one would otherwise be entitled to.

2. Richard Stim, 2nd ed. (Berkeley, CA: Nolo, 2016), 381.

CHAPTER 5

1. *Non-durable* means that the Power of Attorney you give to another will terminate if you become incapacitated in some way. Conversely, a *durable* Power of Attorney will continue to have effect if you become incapacitated.

CHAPTER 7

1. *Pro-rata* means prorated. So, if the artist performs only half of the contracted performance, he is entitled to only half of his fee.

2. *Discovery* means investigating by asking questions and requiring the production of documents.

3. *On the merits*, in this instance, means the opportunity to present your case to the arbitrator.

CHAPTER 8

1. M. William Krasilovsky and Sydney Shemel, *This Music Business: The Definitive Guide to the Business and Legal Issues of the Music Industry*, 10th ed. (New York: Watson-Guptill, 2007).

2. Per the Association of Talent Agents; see http://www.agentassociation.com.

3. For more information about the approach each state takes to regulating agents and managers, see www.napama.org/legal.

4. NY General Business Law §190.

5. www.agentassociation.com

6. www.ncopm.com

7. www.napama.org

8. A covenant is a promise.

Index

About the Author

Before deciding upon law school, David Williams worked simultaneously as an underwriter in Manhattan's financial district and as an assistant to an artist manager. After law school, he assumed various roles of increasing responsibility, specializing in the drafting and interpretation of professional liability contracts.

In 2002 he launched a part-time consultancy practice, now known as Enterprising Artist Consulting (www.EnterprisingArtistConsulting.com), helping musicians, actors, and other creative people with contract-related matters. Soon, Williams was invited to speak on topics relating to performers' contracts at the Seagle Music Colony, Tanglewood, the American Singers Opera Project, the Crane School of Music, the Manhattan School of Music, the New England Conservatory, the University of Wisconsin-Madison, and Yale, among other institutions. In 2015 he left the corporate setting to dedicate himself to this work full-time.

Williams holds a JD from New York Law School and degrees in vocal performance from the University of Wisconsin-Madison (DMA) and the New England Conservatory of Music (MM), as well as a BM in Musical Studies from the Crane School of Music at SUNY Potsdam where he recently taught Music Law as an adjunct professor at the Crane Institute for Music Business and Entrepreneurship.

He currently serves as Company Manager at TriCities Opera in Binghamton, New York and can be reached at legaldavid@gmail.com.

CPSIA information can be obtained
at www.ICGtesting.com
Printed in the USA
BVOW08s1638261017
498739BV00001B/3/P